D1311501

SPANISH BAR & RESTAURANT COOKING

SPANISH BAR & RESTAURANT COOKING

DELICIOUS AND AUTHENTIC RECIPES FOR PAELLA, TAPAS AND SANGRIA

NATALIA SOLÍS BALLINGER AND MARIA SOLÍS BALLINGER

APPLE

A QUINTET BOOK

Published by Apple Press
Sheridan House
112-116A Western Road
Hove
East Sussex BN3 1DD

Copyright © 2003 Quintet Publishing Limited

All rights reserved. No part of this work may be reproducedor transmitted
in any form or by any means—graphic, electronic or mechanical, including
photocopying,recording, taping or information storage and retrieval
systems—without the prior written permission of the copyright holder.

ISBN 1-84092-411-X

This book was produced and designed by
Quintet Publishing Limited
6 Blundell Street
London N7 9BH

Project Editor: Clare Tomlinson
Editor: Anna Bennett
Art Director: Sharanjit Dhol
Designer: Janis Utton
Photographer: Ian Garlick
Food Stylist: Christine Rodriguez
Creative Director: Richard Dewing
Publisher: Oliver Salzmann

Manufactured in Singapore by PICA Digital (Pte) Ltd.
Printed in China by Leefung-Asco Printers Ltd.

CONTENTS

INTRODUCTION

The Cuisine of Spain

The delicate interplay between history and geography in Spain has resulted in one of the most unique and intriguing cuisines the world has to offer. Spanish cuisine has been shaped by the country's landscape, climate, and a diversity of cultures, creating a rewarding and varied culinary legacy that includes everything from fresh grains and home-grown vegetables to delectable seafood and tender red meat. It is a cuisine that is at once sophisticated, yet basic, unadorned, and elegant.

The elegance of Spanish cuisine lies in its simplicity. Fresh ingredients, strong flavors, and unpretentious presentation lie at the heart of any successful Spanish dish. Chefs in Spain eschew the practice of overloading a dish with ingredients, preferring instead to let the true flavors shine through. Food is not hidden under heavy sauces, nor is its essence suffocated beneath layers of unnecessary seasonings. Rather, Spanish cuisine relies on the subtlety of the Mediterranean olive oil, garlic, and fresh herbs.

The history of Spanish cooking has its roots in Spain's turbulent history. The Roman conquest resulted in the introduction of olive oil and garlic to the Iberian Peninsula. The Romans left their culinary mark through the introduction of cooking methods like roasting, grilling, and baking. Their most important contribution, however, was the introduction of vast irrigation systems, which paved the way for the successful introduction of vegetables, fruits, and grains from other regions of the world. The Visigoths subsequently introduced livestock farming, and brought spinach, radishes, and some beans into the area.

Spain's cuisine was not completely revolutionized, however, until the Moorish conquest of 711. Occupying the country for more than seven centuries, the Moors left an indelible influence on the country's poetry, art, music, dance, language, architecture, and, notably, food. When the Moors conquered Spain, they brought with them almonds, rice, sugar, aubergines (eggplants), citrus fruits, and spices, all of which have become fundamental to Spanish cuisine. The Arabic words for many of these ingredients are reflected in various vocabularies of Spain to this day—the Spanish *arroz* (rice) is nearly identical to the Arabic *arruz*; *naranja* (orange) is practically the twin of the Arabic *naranya*; saffron, *azafran*, is directly derived from the Arabic *aza'faran*; and *azucar* (sugar) is the remnant of the Arabic *az-zukker*.

The Moorish occupation also infused the peninsula's cuisine with a certain sophistication. The Moors introduced sweet flavors into main-course dishes, as witnessed in the pairing of meat dishes with citrus fruits, as well as the concept of frying. The invaders abhorred the Iberian practice of loading all of a meal's food on to one plate, instead imposing their subdivision of meals into separate courses, ending with dessert. After the Christian *Reconquista* and the expulsion of the Moors in 1492, Spain's discovery of the New World resulted in the introduction of potatoes, tomatoes, peppers, and courgettes (zucchini) to Spain's culinary repertoire.

While history may have been the most significant influence on Spanish cuisine, the effects of the country's geography also play a crucial role. Spain covers landscapes as varied as wide arid plains, lush fruit groves, magnificent coasts, inhospitable mountain ranges, and dense green forests. It is not surprising, then, that each of Spain's regions yields different recipes and methods of preparation that are unique to each region.

The cool, damp northern regions of Galicia and Asturias, for example, yield signature dishes that are hearty and filling, typical of cold-climate cuisines. Abutting the Atlantic Ocean, these areas enjoy an outstanding reputation for the quality of their seafood. Ranging from octopus to cod, the seafood of Galicia and Asturias is unsurpassed, and tastes especially delectable when paired with Galicia's white *albariño* wine. A dry, crisp white *albariño* is the perfect accompaniment to the region's famous *empanadas*.

The nearby Basque region provides what many believe is the best cuisine of the entire country. Relying on basic ingredients and flavors, Basque chefs are unique in their creation of refined sauces. The area's cuisine takes full advantage of the abundant and varied seafood yielded by the Atlantic Ocean, along with the fine cattle grazing in the mountains.

In the south, Andalucía reflects Spain's vibrant Moorish past more than any other province. It is here that olive trees grow, spurting up in uniform rows as far as the eye can see. Andalucía is the Spain of the popular imagination, with sun-drenched white villages, unrelenting sun, and golden sandy beaches. It is the Spain of Carmen, Don Juan, and the Barber of Seville. The region is also the birthplace of gazpacho and tapas. Along with Andalucía, the cuisines of Valencia and Murcia also bear the heavy imprint of Spain's Moorish roots, evident in the generous use of citrus fruits and rice in regional favorites.

In contrast, Catalan cuisine bears little resemblance to that of the Moorish conquerors. Bordering the Mediterranean, the northern region of Catalonia is a magical mix of mountains and water. This combination has given birth to a cuisine that fuses meat and poultry with fish and seafood. Catalonia has also gained recognition for its excellent *cavas* (sparkling wines).

It is impossible to capture the essence of this country's rewarding cuisine with mere words. Spanish cuisine must be experienced. As the Spanish say, life is short—eat well.

Gazpacho

During its long, arid summers, Andalucía cools itself down with chilled *gazpacho*, a hearty and pungent soup that has gained fame throughout the world for its amazing thirst-quenching quality. Often described as a "liquid salad," *gazpacho* descends from an ancient Roman concoction based on a combination of stale bread, garlic, olive oil, salt, and vinegar. As the Romans labored to build roads and aqueducts across Spain in the scorching heat, this creamy soup replenished them with the necessary salt and vitamins lost through physical exertion. Later, shepherds and farmers added vegetables to make it more hearty and satisfying. Because tomatoes and peppers were not indigenous to Spain, these ingredients were not added to the soup until after Spain's discovery of the New World. Since that time, *gazpacho* has remained relatively unchanged—an unpretentious soup designed to quench the thirst evoked by the unrelenting Spanish sun.

The origin of the word *gazpacho* is debatable, although scholars believe it may have derived from the word *caspa*, meaning "fragments" or "leftovers." Such an explanation rings true as *gazpacho* is the perfect vehicle for transforming leftovers into a satisfying summer dish.

Traditional *gazpacho* recipes are based on a mixture of ripe tomatoes, peppers, cucumbers, moistened bread, olive oil, garlic, and vinegar. There is no single recipe for the soup, however, as Spanish cooks are wont to throw in whatever vegetables they have on hand or that strike their fancy. The results are nevertheless always impressive.

Delightful local variations of *gazpacho* abound. Eastern Andalucía serves creamy white versions deemed to be Moorish adaptations of the basic recipe. *Ajo blanco* (see page 41), perhaps the best-known of these, hails from the coastal city of Malaga. Meaning literally "white garlic," *ajo blanco* is made with garlic, white bread, oil, vinegar, and almonds.

Huelva tends to favor a green *gazpacho*, which relies on green vegetables and chopped herbs for its flavor. The richest, heaviest *gazpacho*, however, hails from Cordoba. *Salmorejo*, a concentrated variation of *gazpacho*, does not contain the peppers, cucumbers, or other mixed vegetables featured in other recipes. Instead, *salmorejo* relies solely on tomatoes for its thick, distinctive taste. It is often garnished with strips of ham and chopped, hard-cooked eggs.

Contrary to what many outside Spain believe, *gazpacho* is not to be served as an appetizer. Rather, this soup should be served along with the main course, or even afterward. Some Spanish homes even offer *gazpacho* in a glass, to accompany the meal as a beverage. Regardless of when or how it is served, however, *gazpacho* provides the perfect, cooling accompaniment for a steaming Spanish evening.

Tapas

Often defined as bite-sized Spanish hors-d'oeuvres, tapas are more than just appetizers: tapas are a celebration of the Spanish way of life. From the most arid villages of Andalusía to the sophisticated cities of Catalonia, tapas bars, bodegas, and tascas come alive with laughter and boisterous crowds in the early evenings. Friends gather over succulent morsels of food and chilled sherry to laugh, argue, flirt or merely recap their day. After lingering to enjoy a *racion* (portion) or two of tasty bar fare, a group will relinquish their table and meander to another tapas tavern, where they will again converse over a platter of tantalizing snacks. This convivial ritual is deeply woven into Spain's social tapestry.

The tapas tradition dates back many centuries. The most popular explanation of their origin suggests that tapas were born when inn-keepers began placing saucers or pieces of bread atop their customers' wine glasses to prevent flies from swarming in. The word *tapa* means "cover" or "lid." Because a portion of food placed on the dish or slab of bread helped attract more tavern-goers, inn-keepers began to out-do themselves creating new bite-sized "covers," unwittingly sparking a Spanish culinary tradition.

Tapas' amazing versatility, as well as the ease of their preparation, has propelled tapas beyond the borders of Spain and into the forefront of popular cuisine.

Paella

Gastronomically speaking, nothing says Spain better than a paella. It is perhaps fitting that paella stands as the culinary head of Spain; it is fusion cooking at its finest, with influences down the centuries from the Romans and the Moors. Reflecting a nation made up of many cultures, the modern paella is an amalgamation of rice and tasty morsels of seafood, meats, and vegetables that makes an exotic, full-flavored dish, inspired and influenced by so many invasions. The Romans introduced the shallow pan, later used to cook paella, to the Iberian peninsula. The very word paella is derived from the Latin name for a shallow pan, *patella*. The Moors, for their part, introduced rice and saffron to Valencia in the eighth century, without which none of this would be possible.

In the centuries that followed, the peasants of Valencia used the flat Roman pan to cook rice with any ingredients the countryside had to offer: land snails, chicken, rabbit, and seasonal vegetables all found their way into the paella pan. The dish began as a poor man's meal prepared over an open outdoor fire. They would sit in a circle around the fire and eat the rice directly from the pan. The communal nature of this dish thus harks back to its very origins. Little by little, paella gained a reputation outside Valencia and, by the nineteenth century, *paella valenciana* was a countrywide phenomenon.

Nearly every region of Spain and, indeed, practically every household, now has its own version of paella. In fact, it has even been said that the only constant in a good Spanish paella is the rice. Some food critics have scoffed at the regions' disparate and inconsistent treatment of paella, complaining that such varying preparations dilute the dish's purity. But such regional variations of the dish create a delightful exploration for the chef and connoisseur alike. Instead of paella growing stagnant or, worse, being swept under the rug as mere "tourist food," it has been embraced by Spanish provinces and families who have altered the dish to make it distinctly their own. The classic Valencian paella is nonetheless a reliable and steady staple for Spaniards and visitors alike. Surprisingly, this most famous version of paella contains no seafood at all. An authentic Valencian paella does not mix meat with fish or shellfish, and typically consists of rice, chicken, rabbit or pork, beans, olive oil, tomatoes, saffron, and land snails. A taste of this classic paella, prepared outdoors over a crackling fire of citrus trimmings, will transport the diner back through the centuries, when the Valencian shepherds threw what ingredients they could find into the pan, creating a nourishing and delicious dish to sustain them through their labors.

A successful paella depends on many factors. Plump and flavorful rice is a must. It is crucial that the paella's other ingredients do not suffocate the rice, but rather infuse it with subtle flavor. A good paella rice will absorb the exact amount of liquid in which it is cooked, leaving each grain of rice delicately flavored, yet separate. As such, a short-grain rice that absorbs the flavors of the accompanying ingredients is ideal. It is also important not to overseason the rice with salt. If the broth is sufficiently salty, it may not be necessary to add any salt to the dish at all.

Proper use of the paella pan is another decisive factor.

Paella pans must be wide, round, and shallow to ensure that the rice is cooked in a thin layer. It is important to spread the rice out over the entire base of the pan, as this is where most of the dish's flavor resides. Many paella cooks prefer iron pans to stainless steel ones, though both work quite well. If you do not wish to invest in an expensive pan, a shallow casserole should also be effective.

Readers favoring the traditional iron pans must be careful to avoid the iron's inevitable rusting. To avoid this, boil a sprinkling of vinegar and water in the pan before it is first used, then rub the pan's surface with olive oil after it dries.

It is also important to use the proper-sized pan. A 12-inch (30-cm) pan will contain enough rice to serve from two to three people; a 16-inch (40-cm) pan will accommodate from four to five people; a 20-inch (50-cm) pan is suitable for six to eight people; and for those serving from eight to fifteen people, a 26-inch (65-cm) pan works best. Larger paella pans also exist—some, made for festivals, are as wide as 13 feet (39 m), and can feed hundreds of ravenous festival-goers!

Genuine saffron is also necessary for a successful, authentic paella. Although substitutes for saffron, such as paprika, suffice as replacements for the paella's rich yellow color, such substitutes cannot replicate the unique taste that only saffron provides. Saffron is undoubtedly expensive, but a little bit does go a long way, and if it is stored in a dry place away from light, it will keep for up to three years.

Although paellas were traditionally prepared outdoors over an open fire, those preparing paella in modern kitchens can still achieve delectable results. But there are a couple of points to bear in mind. First, an indoor cook will need to use a heat source as large as the paella pan itself. If the largest burner on your stove is too small, straddle the pan over two burners, rotating it regularly to distribute the heat evenly. If need be, the paella may even be cooked outside on

a large gas or charcoal barbecue. If, however, the only heat source available is smaller than the pan, stir the rice at least three times during the first 15 to 20 minutes of cooking, then leave it undisturbed for the remaining cooking time.

Second, to create a paella that tastes of the outdoors, one must simulate the *socarrat*, which is one of the most delightful results of cooking paella over an open fire. One taste of *socarrat*, the crisp, golden rice that sticks to the base and sides of the pan, and one will achieve paella nirvana! Although *socarrat* naturally results only when the paella is cooked over an outdoor flame, indoor cooks can create this delicacy by turning up the heat in the final minutes of cooking until the rice lining the bottom of the pan turns crisp.

Paella should not be served in individual dishes but, as the Spanish still do—straight from the pan. The prepared dish, still steaming, is set in the middle of the table, and diners eat communally from the pan. In Spain, what you eat is only secondary to the people with whom you eat. No meal is complete without convivial company and conversation, and a paella, shared with friends, is the perfect dish for this.

Sangría

Sangría sprang into existence when Spanish bar owners recognized the need for a thirst-quenching summertime drink to refresh their parched patrons. Because straight red wine does not quench thirst, an alternative, lighter beverage was needed. Wine with soda water was a start, but ultimately not very exciting. Combining red wine with juice and fruit and serving it over ice, however, made for a balanced refreshment that was both flavorful and easy to drink. Sangría grew in popularity and spread from bar to bar. Today, it is served in nearly every bar throughout Spain.

As is the case with so many Spanish specialties, there is no fixed recipe for sangría. It consists of "a little bit of this, a little bit of that," and whatever fruits happen to be in the kitchen. That said, this book offers ten "blueprints" for exciting variations on this drink. Feel free to add other ingredients to taste. Because the success of any sangría will depend on the quality of these ingredients, it is crucial always to use fresh fruit and flavorful juice.

Sangría must always be served ice-cold. If serving from a punch bowl, stir the sangría in the bowl before ladling it into a glass. Finally, if possible, drink sangría on the beach— there is no finer feeling.

Festivals

Las Fallas: *Valencia's Festival of Fire*

One of Spain's most exuberant festivals, Las Fallas takes place each March in Valencia. For nearly a week, the city is converted into a noisy parade of smoke bombs, firecrackers, dance, and song. Valencia's streets, balconies, and plazas swell with locals, tourists, and, most importantly, fire fighters—for this fiesta culminates in a massive festival of fireworks and flames.

The "Fallas," for which the festival is named, are giant papier-mâché figures. Sometimes grotesque and often humorous, there tend to be many caricatures of Spanish political figures. On the final night of this grand fiesta, *La Nit del Foc*, each Falla is torched, resulting in spectacular, stories-high flames that engulf the city. On any given night during this fiesta, Valencia's streets are flooded with music and laughter, while the aroma of paella wafts through the air.

People often set up their paella pans on the streets, creating heaping portions of the savory rice dish to feed the noisy throngs of festival-goers.

A noisy swirl of color, flame, and excitement, *Las Fallas* is an exuberant festival that everyone should see at least once.

La Tomatina: *The World's Largest Food Fight*

Only 30 miles (48 km) west of Valencia, the sleepy Spanish town of Buñol is normally quite tidy. All this drastically changes, however, on the day of the Tomatina. Since 1944, on the last Wednesday of August each year, this sleepy little town has become home to the world's largest food fight. At least 20,000 thrill-seekers hurl approximately 150,000 tomatoes at one another as Buñol's main square, the Plaza del Pueblo, erupts in a fiery blaze of tomato wars. All the participants must abide by a fixed set of rules: they may only hurl tomatoes, the tomatoes must be squished before they are hurled, and tearing of the other players' clothes is forbidden.

La Tomatina is the culmination of the town's week-long festival honoring its patron saint, San Luis Bertrán. During the festival, Buñol is filled with music, parties, parades, and fireworks. On the eve of the tomato battle, the town's best paella cooks hold their own unofficial paella contest. The unmistakable scent of saffron fills the air as the many paella pans line the narrow medieval streets leading to the Plaza del Pueblo. Revelers fill up on the delicious paella to fortify themselves for the following day's messy tomato war.

The Carnaval del Toro of Ciudad Rodrigo

The phrase "the running of the bulls" usually conjures up Hemingway-inspired images of Pamplona in the minds of most people. However, many other Spanish villages also host their own runnings of bulls festivals. One of these, Ciudad Rodrigo's Carnaval del Toro, dates from the fifteenth century and is one of Spain's oldest bull festivals. Perhaps the most stunning spectacle of the festival is the parade of horses, where expert horsemen drive the bulls into the city from the countryside.

Food and drink abound. Festival-goers enjoy chorizo sausage, Spanish tortilla, thick beef stew, and jugs of red wine. Thick country bread, handed out by the fistful, helps prevent the deluge of wine from going to one's head.

SALMÓN CON ESPÁRRAGOS

Asparagus Wrapped in Smoked Salmon

This elegant tapa is as simple to prepare as it is to eat. Always popular with guests, salmon-wrapped asparagus spears are delicious yet light, perfect if a hearty paella is to be served later in the evening. The alioli (garlic mayonnaise) makes the accompaniment, either spooned over the asparagus, or served on the side as a dip. This recipe yields a generous portion of the creamy sauce, so make sure to have plenty of fresh bread on hand to mop up any remaining alioli. Raw eggs should not be consumed by pregnant women or people with weak immune systems. If refrigerated, the alioli will keep for 24 hours.

SERVES 6 • 20 MINUTES PREPARATION • 10 MINUTES COOKING

6 cloves garlic, chopped fine

Pinch of salt

3 medium egg yolks

1 teaspoon white wine vinegar

2 cups (16 fl. oz/450 ml) olive oil

Lemon juice, to taste

24 asparagus spears

6 slices smoked salmon

1 First, make the alioli. Using a mortar and pestle, pound the garlic and salt together until they form a smooth paste. One by one, thoroughly beat in the egg yolks. Mix in the vinegar. Slowly add the olive oil, drop by drop at first, increasing to a thin stream and stirring constantly once the mixture begins to thicken and emulsify. Sprinkle with lemon juice to taste. Refrigerate while preparing the rest of the dish.

2 Wash and trim the asparagus spears. Bring 1 cup (8 fl. oz/225 ml) water to a boil and steam the asparagus, covered, for 4 minutes or until tender. Refresh the asparagus in iced water and blot dry with paper towels.

3 Cut each slice of salmon in half lengthwise, to yield 12 slices. Then cut each of the 12 slices in half crosswise, to yield 24 slices of salmon. Wrap each piece of salmon around each asparagus spear, making sure to leave the tip exposed. If serving as finger food, the salmon can be secured in place with a toothpick.

4 Arrange the asparagus attractively on a serving platter. The alioli may either be spooned over the asparagus, or served on the side as a dip.

PIPERADA

Basque-style Eggs

Piperada is a filling egg dish, which makes a delicious brunch, and it can also be served as a tapa. A popular variation of this recipe serves the piperada on toasted bread rounds dripping with butter. Either way, this simple egg dish is sure to become a part of your culinary repertoire.

SERVES 3 TO 4 • 10 MINUTES PREPARATION • 20 MINUTES COOKING

4 tablespoons olive oil

2 small onions, peeled and diced fine

1 medium green pepper, seeded and sliced into thin strips

1 medium red pepper, seeded and sliced into thin strips

2 cloves garlic, peeled and minced

1 slice cured ham, cut into strips

2 large tomatoes, chopped

Salt and pepper, to taste

4 eggs

Chopped parsley, to garnish

1 Heat the oil in a pan and sauté the onions, peppers, and garlic until tender. Fold in the ham and tomatoes, and season with salt and pepper. Continue to heat until the vegetables are almost cooked.

2 Lightly beat the eggs with a fork. Pour the eggs over the vegetables and cook over low heat until the eggs are thick but still soft. Transfer to an earthenware dish, garnish with parsley, and serve warm.

ACEITUNAS ALIÑADAS

Marinated Green Olives

Green olives marinated in herbs and garlic always seem to be at hand at any Spanish establishment. Served with toasted, salted almonds and often accompanying a frothy beer, these olives especially evoke the taste of Spain.

MAKES 1 POUND (450G) • 10 MINUTES PREPARATION • 3-7 DAYS MARINATING

2 cups (16 oz/450 g) unpitted large green Spanish olives

7 cloves garlic, peeled and minced

2 bay leaves

$^1/_2$ medium lemon, sliced

1 teaspoon dried oregano

1 teaspoon ground fennel seeds

$^1/_2$ teaspoon dried thyme

$^1/_2$ teaspoon ground cumin seeds

$^1/_2$ teaspoon dried rosemary

$^1/_2$ teaspoon Spanish paprika

$^1/_2$ teaspoon black pepper

TO SERVE

Toasted almonds

Bread

1 Lightly crush the olives with a mallet, or make slight slits on each olive with a knife, to ensure that the marinade permeates them. Place the olives in a sealable glass jar and add the remaining ingredients. Fill the jar with water and shake well. Marinate at room temperature for several days to a week.

2 Serve the olives with toasted almonds and fresh bread.

ENSALADILLA

Spanish Potato Salad

This traditional tapa is served throughout every region of Spain, with little variation. A poorly made version will taste like a mouthful of mayonnaise. On the other hand, a well-made ensaladilla is a perfectly balanced mixture of potatoes, hard-cooked eggs, and vegetables, using the mayonnaise solely to accent these other flavors. This colorful salad is served at nearly every tapas bar; it is even served free at times with an order of beer.

SERVES 4 • 15 MINUTES PREPARATION • 30 MINUTES COOKING

3 medium (16 oz/450 g) potatoes

1 large (3 oz/85 g) carrot, diced

5 tablespoons shelled green peas

2/3 cup (4 oz/115 g) green beans

1/2 medium onion, chopped

1 small red pepper, chopped

4 cocktail gherkins, sliced

2 tablespoons baby capers

12 anchovy-stuffed olives

1 hard-cooked egg, sliced thin

2/3 cup (5fl. oz/150 ml) mayonnaise

1 tablespoon lemon juice

1 teaspoon Dijon mustard

Freshly ground black pepper, to taste

Chopped fresh parsley, to garnish

1 In a saucepan, cook the potatoes and carrot in lightly salted water. Bring to a boil and allow to simmer until almost tender. Fold in the peas and beans, and cook until all the vegetables are tender. Drain the vegetables and transfer them into a serving platter. Add the onion, pepper, gherkins, capers, olives, and egg slices.

2 In a separate bowl, thoroughly combine the mayonnaise, lemon juice, and mustard. Add this mixture to the serving platter, mixing well to ensure all the ingredients are coated. Sprinkle with pepper and toss. Garnish with chopped parsley and refrigerate. Allow to stand at room temperature for about 1 hour immediately before serving to enhance the salad's flavor. As any dish made with mayonnaise, ensaladilla should be refrigerated and will not keep for more than 1 to 2 days.

TAPAS AND GAZPACHO

GAZPACHO ORIENTAL

Eastern-influenced Gazpacho

This dish demonstrates how each chef can put his own unique stamp on a gazpacho recipe. This particular gazpacho has distinctively Eastern undercurrents, as evidenced by the use of soy sauce, lo mein noodles, and rice vinegar. Not surprisingly, this blending of cultures yields delicious results!

SERVES 6 TO 8 • 15 MINUTES PREPARATION PLUS CHILLING TIME

$1/4$ cup (2 fl. oz/50 ml) olive oil

$1/4$ cup (2 fl. oz/50 ml) rice vinegar

6 ripe medium tomatoes, halved

1 medium cucumber

1 medium courgette (zucchini)

1 medium green pepper, seeded and chopped

1 cup (8 fl. oz/230 ml) vegetable broth

2 teaspoons soy sauce

$1/8$ teaspoon Tabasco sauce

TO GARNISH

Finely chopped spring onions

Canned lo mein noodles

1 Process the olive oil, vinegar, half of the tomatoes, the cucumber, the courgette, half the green peppers and $1/2$ cup (4 fl. oz/125 ml) of the vegetable broth in a blender or food processor and transfer to a large bowl. Add the remaining vegetables and vegetable broth to the blender, process, and transfer to the large bowl. Pass the contents of the bowl through a sieve (if you prefer you can dilute the mixture with water). Add the soy sauce and Tabasco sauce, stir well, and refrigerate until chilled.

2 Immediately before serving, sprinkle the soup with the spring onions and lo mein noodles.

PATATAS BRAVAS

Crisp Spiced Potatoes

Patatas bravas is a basic, traditional tapa as popular in elegant big-city establishments as it is in the more modest village hostelries. As with most tapas, each bar and household will have its own recipe, naturally believed to the best! Savor this mildly tangy version of patatas bravas with a chilled white wine.

SERVES 4 • 10 MINUTES PREPARATION • 20 MINUTES COOKING

3 tablespoons olive oil

2 tablespoons minced onion

2 cloves garlic, minced

1 1/2 tablespoons Spanish paprika

1/4 tsp Tabasco sauce

1/4 tsp ground thyme

1/2 cup (4 fl. oz/120 ml) ketchup

1/2 cup (4 fl. oz/120 ml) mayonnaise

Salt and freshly ground black pepper

4 large Russet potatoes, peeled and cut into 1-inch (2.5-cm) cubes

1 cup (8 fl. oz/240 ml) olive oil, for frying

Chopped parsley, to garnish

1 In a saucepan, heat 3 tablespoons olive oil over medium heat. Add the onion and garlic and sauté until the onion is soft. Turn off the heat, and add the paprika, Tabasco sauce, and thyme, stirring well. Transfer to a bowl and add the ketchup and mayonnaise. Season with salt and pepper to taste. Set aside.

2 Sprinkle the potatoes lightly with salt. In a large pan, fry the potatoes in 1 cup (8 fl. oz/225 ml) olive oil until cooked through and golden-brown, stirring occasionally. (Take care when adding the potatoes to the saucepan because the oil will splatter due to the salt.) Drain the potatoes on paper towels, check the seasoning, add more salt if necessary, and set aside.

3 Mix the potatoes with the sauce immediately before serving to ensure that the potatoes retain their crispness. Garnish with chopped parsley and serve warm.

ALBÓNDIGAS CON SALSA DE TOMATE

Meatballs in Tomato Sauce

Found in most tapas bars, this traditional dish tastes best when served piping hot straight from the pan. Provide plenty of fresh bread to mop up the juicy tomato sauce.

SERVES 3 TO 4 • 15 MINUTES PREPARATION • 30 MINUTES COOKING

8 oz (225 g) ground beef

1 cup (2 oz/75 g) fresh white breadcrumbs

2 tablespoons grated **Manchego** or **Parmesan** cheese

1 tablespoon tomato paste

3 cloves garlic, chopped fine

2 scallions, chopped fine

1 egg, beaten

2 teaspoons chopped fresh thyme

$1/2$ teaspoon turmeric

Salt and pepper, to taste

2 tablespoons olive oil

2 cups (16 oz/450 g) canned plum tomatoes, chopped

2 tablespoons red wine

2 teaspoons chopped fresh basil leaves

2 teaspoons chopped fresh rosemary

1 In a bowl, thoroughly mix together the beef, breadcrumbs, cheese, tomato paste, garlic, scallions, egg, thyme, turmeric, salt, and pepper. Using your hands, shape the mixture into 12 to 15 firm balls.

2 Heat the olive oil in a pan over medium-high heat. Add the meatballs and cook for several minutes or until browned on all sides.

3 Add the tomatoes, wine, basil, and rosemary. Simmer gently for around 20 minutes, or until the meatballs are cooked. Season generously with salt and pepper and serve hot.

EMPANADILLAS DE ATÚN Y DE QUESO

Tuna and Goat Cheese Empanadillas

Empanadas are crisp turnovers that can be filled with anything from ham and cheese to spinach and pine nuts, or the previous day's leftovers. Although they are often associated with South America, empanadas originated in Spain's northwestern region of Galicia, where they remain immensely popular to this day. Empanadillas, the smaller, pocket-size versions of empanadas, are generally served as tapas, and, because no silverware is required to eat them, make perfect party food.

SERVES 6 TO 8 • 30 MINUTES PREPARATION • 35 MINUTES COOKING

1 tablespoon olive oil

5 tablespoons minced onion

2 cloves garlic, minced

6 oz (175 g) canned tuna, packed in olive oil

1/2 cup (4 oz/115 g) goat cheese

1/3 cup (3 oz/85 g) pimento-stuffed olives, chopped

5 tablespoons toasted pine nuts

5 tablespoons capers, chopped

1 teaspoon paprika

Salt and pepper, to taste

16 oz (450 g) puff pastry, defrosted if frozen

1 Heat the olive oil in a pan over medium heat. Add the onion and garlic and sauté for about 5 minutes or until softened. Remove from the heat and set aside.

2 Using a fork, mash the tuna with the onion, garlic, goat cheese, olives, pine nuts, capers, paprika, salt, and pepper. Set aside.

3 On a floured surface, roll out the pastry to 1/8-inch (3-mm) thickness. Using a 3-inch (7.5-cm) cookie cutter, cut out as many dough circles as the dough will allow, rerolling the dough sheets if necessary. Cupping each dough round in your hand, spoon about 1 teaspoon of the filling into the center of each dough round, then brush the edges with a little water. Fold the dough over the mixture to form a crescent. Pinch the edges of crescent to seal the dough closed. Use the back of a fork to further press the edges of the dough together.

4 Transfer to a greased baking sheet, and repeat the process with the remaining dough rounds and pastry. Bake in the oven at 400 °F (200 °C) for 20 to 25 minutes or until golden. Allow to cool for 5 minutes before serving.

ENSALADA DE CEBOLLA Y NARANJAS

Red Onion and Orange Salad

This popular and colorful salad lends a festive note to any tapas table, and is featured in many tapas bars throughout Spain. Some versions omit the red onion, or replace the raspberry vinegar with lemon juice. No matter which variation is served, however, this salad is tangy and refreshing on a hot summer day, and should always be served chilled.

SERVES 4 • 15 MINUTES PREPARATION

4 ripe medium oranges, peeled

1 small red onion, sliced fine

2 tablespoons raspberry vinegar

6 tablespoons extra-virgin olive oil

Salt and freshly ground pepper

4 tablespoons sultanas, covered for 20 mins in hot water, then drained

20 black olives, pitted

2 tablespoons sunflower seeds

2 tablespoons almonds, blanched and chopped fine

Sprigs of fresh mint, to garnish

1 Remove the white pith from the oranges and cut the fruit crosswise into 1/4-inch (5-mm) slices. Arrange on a serving platter and scatter over the sliced red onion.

2 In a small bowl, whisk together the vinegar, olive oil, salt, and pepper. Spoon this dressing over the onion and oranges. Sprinkle with the raisins, olives, sunflower seeds, and almonds. Garnish with mint sprigs and serve chilled.

Red Onion and Orange Salad

ACEITUNAS ALIÑADAS CON AJO

Garlic-marinated Black Olives

Attesting to the simplicity of tapas, a handful of marinated olives is often ample accompaniment to a glass of chilled sherry in most Spanish tapas bars. Marinated to piquant perfection, these olives are far from ordinary. To fully develop the flavor of garlic in the recipe below, it is best to allow the olives to marinate for at least several days before serving.

MAKES 8 OZ (225G) • 10 MINUTES PREPARATION • 2–3 DAYS MARINATING TIME

1 cup (8 oz/225 g) black olives

2 dried red chillies

12 cloves garlic, minced

Red wine vinegar, as required

Dash of lemon juice

1 Lightly crush the olives (without breaking them) and pour into a glass jar with a lid, discarding any oil produced. Add the dried chillies and garlic, lightly shaking the jar to ensure equal distribution. Pour in enough red wine vinegar so that the jar's contents are entirely submerged. Add a dash of lemon juice, seal the jar, and store at room temperature for several days, shaking the jar occasionally. Serve the marinated olives with a glass of sherry.

TORTILLA ESPAÑOLA

Spanish Potato Omelette

Along with paella, the ubiquitous Spanish potato omelette is perhaps one of the best-known Spanish dishes. It is impossible to find a self-respecting tapas bar that does not feature tortilla in its repertoire. As delicious as it is versatile, this Spanish staple lends itself to countless variations according to personal taste. Some cooks mix in mushrooms, beans, spinach, and tomatoes, while others choose to omit the onion and instead cover the tortilla in tomato sauce. Others still would never dream of serving the tortilla without heaping mounds of mayonnaise. Each region, and each tapas bar, will have its own variation of the traditional tortilla. This delicious tapa can be served warm or cold.

SERVES 4 • 15 MINUTES PREPARATION • 30 MINUTES COOKING

1 cup (8 fl. oz/240 ml) olive oil

5 medium (40 oz/1.1 kg) baking potatoes, peeled, sliced, and lightly sprinkled with salt

1/2 large yellow onion, chopped

3 cloves garlic, minced

5 eggs

Salt

1 Heat the olive oil in a 9-inch (23-cm) pan and add the potato slices carefully, because the salt will make the oil splatter. Try to keep the potato slices separate so they will not stick together. Cook, turning occasionally, over medium heat for 5 minutes. Add the onions and garlic and cook until the potatoes are tender. Drain into a colander, leaving about 3 tablespoons oil in the pan.

2 Meanwhile, in a large bowl, whisk the eggs with a pinch of salt. Add the potatoes, and stir to coat with the egg. Add the egg-coated potatoes to the very hot oil in the pan, spreading them evenly to completely cover the base of the pan. Lower the heat to medium and continue to cook, shaking the pan frequently, until mixture is half set.

3 Use a plate to cover the pan and invert the omelette away from the hand holding the plate (so as not to burn your hand with any escaping oil). Add 1 tablespoon oil to the pan and slide the omelette back into the pan on its uncooked side. Cook until completely set. Allow the omelette to cool, then cut into wedges. Season with salt and sprinkle with lemon juice to taste. Serve warm or at room temperature.

TAPAS AND GAZPACHO

TAPAS AND GAZPACHO

ESCALIVADA

Catalan Roasted Vegetable Salad

From the Catalan verb escalivar, *meaning "to cook over hot embers," escalivada is a colorful array of vegetables, roasted to perfection and glistening with olive oil. Escalivada is usually served on a rustic, earthenware platter, and, as with most tapas, should be accompanied by thick slices of fresh crusty bread.*

SERVES 4 • 30 MINUTES PREPARATION • 35 MINUTES COOKING

2 medium yellow onions, unpeeled

1 medium (16 oz/450 g) aubergine (eggplant)

1 large green pepper

1 large red pepper

1 large yellow pepper

2 medium tomatoes

8 cloves garlic

2 teaspoons cumin seeds

2 tablespoons lemon juice

3 tablespoons sherry vinegar

1/4 cup (2 fl. oz/60 ml) olive oil

1 teaspoon sweet paprika

1 teaspoon chopped fresh rosemary

Salt, to taste

1 Lay the onions on a baking sheet and bake in the oven at 350 °F (180 °C) for 10 minutes. Add the aubergine and bake for a further 10 minutes. Add the peppers, tomatoes, and half of the garlic cloves and bake until all vegetables are tender. Remove the vegetables from the oven and allow to cool.

2 Peel the vegetables with your fingers. Cut the aubergine into strips. Remove the stem, core, and seeds from the peppers, and cut into strips as well. Seed the tomatoes, then slice into wedges. Thinly slice the onion. Arrange the vegetables attractively on a serving platter.

3 In a food processor, combine the roasted garlic, the remaining cloves of raw garlic, the cumin seeds, lemon juice, vinegar, olive oil, paprika, and rosemary. When the mixture is smooth and uniform, pour it evenly over the vegetables. Season with salt and serve.

ESPINACAS CATALANAS

Catalan Spinach with Raisins and Pine Nuts

Sweet, plump raisins and crisp pine nuts are often paired together in classic Catalan fare. Try them here tossed with fresh spinach and stuffed olives. This traditional combination is excellent as a tapa or as a side dish. As a variation, omit the croutons and serve the spinach on toasted bread slices.

SERVES 4 TO 6 • 10 MINUTES PREPARATION • 20 MINUTES COOKING

3 tablespoons olive oil

2 cloves garlic, minced

1 medium onion, chopped fine

16 cups (32 oz/900 g) spinach

1/2 cup (2 1/2 oz/70 g) dark raisins, soaked in hot water for 20 minutes and drained

4 tablespoons pine nuts

1/4 cup (2 oz/55 g) pimento-stuffed olives, chopped fine

Salt and pepper, to taste

Croutons, to serve

1 Heat the olive oil in a pan. Add the garlic and onion and fry until golden. Set aside.

2 Rinse the spinach and trim the leaves from the stalks. Discard the stalks. Place the spinach in a large saucepan, cover, and cook over low heat for 10 minutes in the water clinging to its leaves. Drain, then stir the spinach into the onion and garlic. Mix in the raisins, pine nuts, and olives. Season generously with salt and pepper. Transfer to a serving dish, sprinkle croutons on top, and serve warm.

CHAMPIÑONES AL AJILLO

Sautéed Mushrooms in Garlic Sauce

Few tapas taste more Spanish than champiñones al ajillo, dripping with olive oil, garlic, and dry Spanish sherry. To make this tapa even more authentic, be sure to serve the mushrooms with plenty of fresh, crusty bread to mop up the delicious juices.

SERVES 4 • 10 MINUTES PREPARATION • 12 MINUTES COOKING

1/4 cup (2 fl. oz/60 ml) olive oil

4 cups (8 oz/250 g) mushrooms, wiped clean and quartered

6 cloves garlic, minced

3 tablespoons dry sherry

2 tablespoons lemon juice

1/2 teaspoon dried red chilli, seeded and crumbled

1/2 teaspoon Spanish paprika

Salt and pepper, to taste

2 tablespoons chopped parsley

1 Heat the oil in a pan and sauté the mushrooms over high heat for about 2 minutes, stirring constantly. Lower the heat to medium and add the garlic, sherry, lemon juice, dried chilli, paprika, and salt and pepper. Cook for about 5 minutes or until the garlic and mushrooms have softened. Remove from the heat, sprinkle with chopped parsley, and serve on small earthenware platters.

ENSALADA DE MANZANA Y NUECES

Apple and Walnut Salad

This refreshing, crisp summer salad provides the perfect accompaniment to a glass (or two) of chilled Spanish sherry. For a tangier version, add a dash of lemon juice to the mayonnaise before mixing the mayonnaise into the salad.

SERVES 2 • 10 MINUTES PREPARATION

1 large sweet green apple

3 tablespoons lemon juice

3 spring onions, chopped

1/4 cup (11/4 oz/35 g) sultanas

1 celery stalk, trimmed and chopped

2 medium cooked potatoes, peeled and chopped

8 walnuts, shelled

1 cup (8 fl. oz/225 ml) mayonnaise

11/4 tablespoons chopped coriander

1 Peel, core, and dice the apple. Sprinkle with a little lemon juice to prevent discoloration and set aside. Combine the spring onions, sultanas, celery, and potatoes in a medium earthenware bowl. Add the diced apple, walnuts, and mayonnaise, mixing thoroughly. Sprinkle lightly with coriander and serve immediately.

Apple and Walnut Salad

TAPAS AND GAZPACHO

PINCHITOS

Spiced Pork Kabobs

Pinchitos, succulent pork skewers, are especially popular in Andalucía, where families grill them outdoors over an open fire. As with many dishes in Andalucía, Moorish influences abound. Here, they are evidenced in the use of cumin and paprika.

SERVES 4 • 15 MINUTES PREPARATION • 15 MINUTES COOKING • 2–3 HOURS MARINATING TIME

$^1/_4$ **cup (2 fl. oz/60 ml) olive oil**

2 cloves garlic, chopped

2 tablespoons lemon juice

2 teaspoons salt

1 teaspoon curry powder

1 teaspoon ground cumin

1 teaspoon turmeric

$^1/_2$ **teaspoon cayenne pepper**

$^1/_2$ **teaspoon paprika**

$^1/_4$ **teaspoon thyme**

16 oz (450 g) lean pork, cut into small cubes

1 In a shallow dish, combine the olive oil, garlic, lemon juice, salt, curry powder, ground cumin, turmeric, cayenne pepper, paprika, and thyme, and mix well. Gently place the pork pieces in the dish and marinate for several hours in the refrigerator. Turn the pork over periodically to ensure that all sides are equally coated.

2 Immediately before grilling, remove the pork pieces from the marinade, and thread them on to skewers. Place the pork skewers on the hot grill, and cook, turning them until the pork is fully cooked on all sides. Serve hot, fresh from the grill.

GAZPACHO ANDALUZ

Classic Andalusian Gazpacho

This basic version of gazpacho is the one travelers would be most likely to encounter when touring through Spain. The fact that this soup is commonly found, however, in no way renders it "ordinary." One taste of this chilled gazpacho and you will be instantly transported to a land of whitewashed walls, red-tiled roofs, and a golden sun.

SERVES 8 · 20 MINUTES PREPARATION PLUS CHILLING TIME

1/2 cup (4 fl. oz/120 ml) olive oil

1/4 cup (2 fl. oz/50 ml) red wine vinegar

3 cloves garlic, chopped

1 tablespoon salt

1/4 teaspoon cumin

1/8 teaspoon Tabasco sauce

4 large ripe tomatoes, sliced

4 cups (32 oz/900 g) canned plum tomatoes

1 medium green pepper, sliced

1 medium cucumber, sliced

1/2 medium yellow onion, sliced

Ice cubes

TO SERVE

Chopped tomatoes

Croutons

Hard-cooked eggs

1 Combine the olive oil, vinegar, garlic, salt, cumin, and Tabasco sauce in a food processor with half of the vegetables listed and purée. Transfer the soup mixture to a large bowl. Purée the remaining vegetables and add to the soup. Add ice cubes (or water) to taste, and additional salt if necessary. Refrigerate until very cool, or overnight.

2 Before serving, garnish the gazpacho with chopped tomatoes, croutons, and hard-cooked eggs.

Classic Andalusian Gazpacho

GAZPACHO VERDE

Green Gazpacho

This colorful variation on the traditional red gazpacho hails from Huelva and the Sierra Morena in Andalucía. Unlike the classic gazpacho recipes, this soup relies on spinach, lettuce, parsley, and mint for its freshness and texture. Although it is quite different from its more traditional gazpacho cousins, this version is every bit as refreshing.

SERVES 4 TO 6 • 15 MINUTES PREPARATION PLUS CHILLING TIME

2 cups (4 oz/115 g) lettuce leaves, chopped

2 cups (4 oz/115 g) spinach

3 spring onions, diced

$1/2$ large cucumber, peeled and diced

1 tablespoon chopped parsley

2 cups (16 fl. oz/475 ml) chicken broth

$1/2$ cup (4 fl. oz/120 ml) sour cream, plus extra to garnish (optional)

$1/2$ cup (4 fl. oz/120 ml) mayonnaise

1 teaspoon chopped fresh mint leaves

$1/2$ teaspoon white pepper

$1/2$ teaspoon salt

1 In a blender, combine the lettuce, spinach, spring onions, cucumbers, and parsley until the mixture forms a purée. Gradually add in the chicken broth, sour cream, mayonnaise, mint, white pepper, and salt. Purée the mixture until it reaches an even consistency. Refrigerate the soup until you are ready to serve.

2 Serve the soup chilled in individual bowls, with a spoonful of sour cream over each serving, if desired.

ALIÑO DE PIMIENTOS ASADOS CON ATÚN

Tapa of Roasted Peppers with Tuna

SERVES 3 TO 4 • 30 MINUTES PREPARATION •

10 MINUTES COOKING

3 medium green peppers

3 medium red peppers

2 large tomatoes, skinned, seeded, and diced

¹/₂ small yellow onion, diced

¹/₂ cup (4 fl. oz/120 ml) olive oil

¹/₃ cup (3 fl. oz/90 ml) red wine vinegar

³/₄ teaspoon salt

¹/₂ teaspoon pepper

2 hard-cooked eggs, shelled and sliced

6 ounces (6 oz/175 g) canned tuna, packed in olive oil

Based on Escalivada (see page 31), this light, refreshing tapa combines ease and elegance in equal parts. The vinaigrette seems almost too easy to prepare, yet it zestily dresses the roasted vegetables to perfection. Oil-infused tuna and hard-cooked eggs add protein to this crisp Mediterranean dish.

1 Char the peppers under a grill until they are blackened on all sides. Wrap in a paper bag and allow to stand for 10 to 15 minutes to steam. Peel, seed, and cut into long, thin strips, then transfer to a bowl. Add the tomatoes and the onion, and set aside.

2 In a medium bowl, whisk together the olive oil, vinegar, salt, and pepper. Pour this mixture over the vegetables and combine well, coating all vegetables with the dressing.

3 Transfer the vegetables to a serving dish and top with the sliced hard-cooked eggs and tuna.

AJO BLANCO

Chilled White Almond Soup

Ajo blanco, a white version of gazpacho, is believed to have originated with the Moors. If a silkier texture is desired, try soaking the blanched almonds in milk before processing. This will enhance the soup's delicate creaminess.

SERVES 4 TO 6 • 15 MINUTES PREPARATION PLUS CHILLING TIME

1 cup (6 oz/170 g) blanched almonds

4 slices crustless white bread, soaked in cold water for 5 minutes

3 garlic cloves, sliced

5 tablespoons olive oil

2 1/2 cups (20 fl. oz/600 ml) cold water

2 tablespoons sherry vinegar

Salt

1/2 cup (3 oz/90 g) seedless green grapes

TO GARNISH

Toasted slivered almonds

Chopped fresh parsley (optional)

1 Combine the almonds, bread, and garlic in a food processor and blend until smooth. With the motor still running, slowly pour in the olive oil until a smooth paste is formed. Add in the cold water and the vinegar. Process until the mixture is thin and smooth. Season with salt to taste.

2 Pour the mixture into a large bowl. Float the grapes on the top of the soup. Cover and allow to chill in the refrigerator. To serve, pour the soup into individual soup bowls and garnish with the toasted almond slivers and chopped parsley, if desired.

GAZPACHO BLANCO

White Gazpacho

This dish is a modern adaptation of Malaga's Ajo blanco (white almond soup—see page 41). Unlike ajo blanco, however, this version omits the almonds and relies on sour cream and yogurt for its unmistakable creamy texture. Almonds are reserved for a crisp garnish.

SERVES 6 • 15 MINUTES PREPARATION PLUS CHILLING TIME

3 medium cucumbers, peeled and chopped

3 cloves garlic, chopped

2 cups (16 fl. oz/470 ml) sour cream

1 cup (8 fl. oz/235 ml) plain yogurt

1 cup (8 fl. oz/ 235 ml) chicken broth

Salt and pepper, to taste

1/8 teaspoon Tabasco sauce

TO GARNISH

Slivered almonds

Seedless green grapes, halved

1 In two batches, purée all the ingredients except for the almonds and grapes in a food processor. Combine both batches in a large bowl and refrigerate for several hours or overnight.

2 Immediately before serving, garnish individual servings with the slivered almonds and grapes.

PAELLA DE ALMEJAS, JAMÓN SERRANO Y CHORIZO

Paella with Clams, Serrano Ham, and Chorizo Sausage

Serrano ham is so adored by the Spanish that it is often served on its own, accompanied by nothing more than a glass of sherry. Savor it here as a flavorful accent to this scrumptious rice. If serrano ham is unavailable, the more readily available Italian prosciutto makes a good substitute.

SERVES 8 • 25 MINUTES PREPARATION • 55 MINUTES COOKING

1/2 cup (4 fl. oz/120 ml) olive oil

1 large onion, chopped

5 cloves garlic, minced

4 oz (115 g) chorizo sausage, crumbled and with casing removed

1 medium red pepper, cut into thin strips

1 medium green pepper, cut into thin strips

2 large tomatoes, skinned, seeded, and chopped

2 cups (18 oz/450 g) rice

41/4 cups (34 fl. oz/1 l) chicken broth

1 teaspoon turmeric

1/4 teaspoon saffron

1/4 teaspoon dried oregano

Salt and pepper, to taste

One 14-oz (400-g) can clams, drained

8 oz (225 g) serrano ham, cut into thin strips

1 tablespoon chopped parsley

Lemon wedges, to serve

1 Heat the oil in a paella pan over medium heat. Add the onion and sauté for about 5 minutes or until the onion begins to soften. Add the garlic and cook for several minutes more. Drop in the chorizo sausage and cook for a further 5 minutes. Mix in the peppers and tomatoes, reduce the heat to low, and cook for a further 10 minutes.

2 Stir in the rice, increase the heat to medium, and sauté for 5 minutes. Pour in the broth, turmeric, saffron, oregano, and salt and pepper to taste, and cook for about 15 minutes. Add in the clams, ham, and parsley and cook for a further 7 minutes, or until all the liquid has been absorbed and the rice is tender. Garnish with lemon wedges and serve.

PAELLA DE ESPÁRRAGOS Y QUESO MANCHEGO

Asparagus and Manchego Cheese Paella

With its distinctive, sharp flavor, Manchego cheese is the most popular sheep's milk cheese in Spain. As its name suggests, Manchego hails from La Mancha, the stomping ground of Cervantes' Don Quixote. Manchego is often savored alone or on a slice of bread. In this dish, the Manchego is grated and enhances the tenderness of the paella's prawns and chicken. Parmesan can be used as an alternative to Manchego.

SERVES 6 • 15 MINUTES PREPARATION • 45 MINUTES COOKING

$1/2$ cup (4 fl. oz/120 ml) olive oil

3 skinless, boneless chicken breasts, cut into chunks

1 large onion, chopped fine

4 cloves garlic, minced

$1^1/2$ cups (12 oz/340 g) rice

2 cups (8 oz/225 g) broccoli florets, cut into bite-size pieces

$3^1/4$ cups (26 fl. oz/770 ml) chicken broth

$1/4$ teaspoon powdered saffron

8 oz (225 g) uncooked prawns

14 oz (400 g) canned asparagus tips

Salt and pepper, to taste

$3/4$ cup ($2^1/2$ oz/70 g) grated Manchego cheese

1 Heat the oil in a paella pan over medium heat. Cook the chicken until browned on all sides. Remove the chicken from the pan and transfer to a dish.

2 Add the onion and garlic to the paella pan, and cook for 2 minutes. Add the rice, broccoli, broth, saffron, prawns, and cooked chicken. Reduce the heat to medium, cover, and cook for a further 20 minutes. Mix in the asparagus tips and salt and pepper to taste. Cook for a further 5 minutes or until the chicken and rice are tender and the broth has been absorbed.

3 Remove the pan from the heat, sprinkle with the Manchego cheese, and serve.

PAELLAS AND ENTRÉES

PAELLA DE GAMBAS Y ALCACHOFAS CON JEREZ

Prawn and Artichoke Paella with Sherry

The use of sherry in this dish evokes the taste of a paella served outdoors in a seaside restaurant. Artichoke hearts provide a flavorful garnish. If you wish, lay lemon wedges around the edge of the rice for an even more attractive presentation.

SERVES 6 • 15 MINUTES PREPARATION • 50 MINUTES COOKING

1/4 cup (2 fl. oz/ 60 ml) olive oil

2 medium onions, chopped

5 cloves garlic, minced

1 small green pepper, diced

1 small red pepper, diced

3 large tomatoes, skinned, seeded, and chopped

1 1/2 cups (12 oz/340 g) rice

2 1/2 cups (20 fl. oz/600 ml) fish broth

1 cup (8 fl. oz/230 ml) sherry

12 oz (340 g) prawns, peeled and deveined

1/2 teaspoon saffron

Salt and pepper, to taste

One 14-oz (400-g) can artichoke hearts, drained

1 Heat the oil in a paella pan over medium heat. Add the onions and garlic and sauté for about 5 minutes, or until onion is soft. Add the peppers and cook for about 5 minutes longer. Add the tomatoes and continue to cook for a further 8 to 10 minutes.

2 Add the rice and cook, stirring, for a further 5 minutes. Mix in the broth, sherry, prawns, saffron, and salt and pepper. Bring to a simmer and cook gently for 20 minutes.

3 Arrange the artichoke hearts on top of the rice and continue cooking until all liquid has been absorbed and the rice is tender, about 5 minutes.

PAELLA CON PASAS Y ALMENDRAS TOSTADAS

Paella with Currants and Toasted Almonds

This unusual recipe, combining chicken with currants and toasted almonds, produces a crisp and succulent rice with just a tinge of sweetness. If you do not have currants on hand, use raisins as a substitute.

SERVES 6 • 20 MINUTES PREPARATION • 40 MINUTES COOKING

2 tablespoons olive oil

2 medium onions, diced

4 cloves garlic, minced

12 oz (350 g) skinless, boneless chicken breasts, cut into small chunks and seasoned with salt and pepper

3^1/$_4$ cups (26 fl. oz/770 ml) chicken broth

^{1}/$_2$ teaspoon saffron

1^1/$_2$ cups (12 oz/340 g) rice

1 cup (8 oz/225 g) currants

Handful of fresh coriander, chopped

Salt and pepper, to taste

^{3}/$_4$ cup (2^1/$_2$ oz/75 g) slivered almonds, toasted

1 Heat the oil in a paella pan over medium heat. Add the onion and garlic and sauté until tender. Add the chicken and cook until lightly browned on all sides, about 5 minutes.

2 At the same time, heat the chicken broth in a small frying pan over low heat. Add the saffron, stir, and keep over low heat until ready for use.

3 Add the rice to the paella pan. Pour in the broth and reduce the heat to low. Cook until the broth has been absorbed and the rice is tender. Remove from the heat and mix in the currants and coriander. Season with salt and pepper, sprinkle with the sliced toasted almonds, and serve.

PAELLA DE RAPE A LA CATALANA

Catalan-style Paella with Monkfish

Hailing from Cataluña, this paella features monkfish, which has gained in popularity in recent years. Prepared and cooked correctly, monkfish looks and tastes like lobster. Here, the subtle flavor and tenderness of the monkfish add the perfect accents to the plump, juicy rice. A chilled white wine is the perfect accompaniment to this seafood paella.

SERVES 6 • 20 MINUTES PREPARATION • 40 MINUTES COOKING

1 cup (8 fl. oz/230 ml) olive oil

24 oz (700 g) monkfish, cut into pieces

1 small chilli

1 slice white bread from a sandwich loaf

5 cloves garlic, minced

2 medium tomatoes, skinned, seeded, and chopped

2 cups (16 oz/450 g) rice

4$1/4$ cups (34 fl. oz/1 l) fish or chicken broth

$1/4$ teaspoon saffron

Salt and pepper, to taste

1 Heat $3/4$ cup (6 fl. oz/175 ml) of the olive oil in a paella pan over medium to high heat. Lightly fry the monkfish pieces all over in the oil and transfer to a platter.

2 In the same oil, sauté the chilli and transfer to a mortar. Fry the slice of bread in the same oil until golden and transfer to the mortar with the chilli. Mash together until a paste is formed.

3 Add the minced garlic and tomatoes to the paella pan and sauté for several minutes. Pour in the remaining oil and, when sufficiently heated, add the rice. Place the monkfish pieces on top, and add the broth, mashed chilli and bread, and the saffron. Cook for 20 to 25 minutes, or until the liquid has been absorbed and the rice is tender.

4 Season with salt and pepper and serve immediately.

PAELLA DE POLLO, CALABACINES Y ROMERO

Paella with Chicken, Courgette, and Rosemary

This deliciously flavored rice dish features tender chicken breasts subtly seasoned with fresh rosemary. It could be said that this paella brings good fortune to those who eat it, for, according to an ancient Spanish superstition, anyone who passes a rosemary bush must pull some sprigs off the fragrant shrub and pocket them to ensure good luck in the week to come. A touch of dry sherry lends this paella extra Andalusian flair.

SERVES 6 • 15 MINUTES PREPARATION • 60 MINUTES COOKING

$3/4$ cup (6 fl. oz/175 ml) olive oil

48 oz (1.3 kg) chicken breasts, boned and cut into pieces

1 large onion, chopped

5 cloves garlic, minced

1 large green pepper, chopped

$1/3$ cup (3 fl. oz/90 ml) dry sherry

$1^1/2$ cups (12 oz/340 g) rice

3 cups (24 fl. oz/700 ml) chicken broth

$1/4$ teaspoon saffron

$1/4$ teaspoon turmeric

3 tablespoons chopped fresh rosemary

3 large courgettes (zucchini), cut into $1^1/2$-inch (4-cm) strips

Salt and pepper, to taste

1 Heat $1/4$ cup (2 fl. oz/50 ml) of the oil in a paella pan. Add the chicken and cook until done and browned on all sides. Set aside.

2 Clean the pan and heat the remaining olive oil over medium heat. Add the onion, and cook for 5 minutes. Add the garlic and green pepper and cook for 3 minutes. Add the sherry and cook for a further 1 minute. Pour in the rice and sauté for 5 minutes. Mix in the broth, saffron, turmeric, browned chicken, and $1^1/2$ tablespoons of the rosemary and cook for 15 minutes.

3 Sprinkle in the remaining rosemary and stir. Arrange the courgettes over the rice, cover, and cook for a further 10 minutes or until the rice and chicken are tender, and the broth has been absorbed. Allow to cool for 5 minutes, and serve.

PAELLA MIXTA

Mixed Seafood, Sausage, and
Chicken Paella

This is the recipe that springs to mind when most people think of paella. While Valencia, the homeland of paella, rarely produces a paella mixing seafood with meat, this paella has caught the popular imagination outside Spain and tends to be the paella served in most Spanish-themed restaurants. It is easy to understand why few could resist the combination of delicate lobster meat, mussels, clams, and prawns teamed with rich chorizo sausage and tender chicken.

SERVES 6 • 30 MINUTES PREPARATION • 60 MINUTES COOKING

10 mussels

10 clams

1/2 cup (4 fl. oz/120 ml), plus 4 tablespoons, olive oil

2 oz (55 g) boneless pork, diced

2 teaspoons minced garlic

3/4 cup (6 oz/170 g) onions, chopped fine

1 medium tomato, skinned, seeded, and chopped

1 small red pepper, seeded and cut into thin strips

1 small green pepper, seeded and cut into thin strips

1 small yellow pepper, seeded and cut into thin strips

32 oz (900 g) skinless, boneless chicken breasts, cut into chunks

Salt and pepper, to taste

1 teaspoon paprika

1/2 teaspoon dried rosemary

1/2 teaspoon dried thyme

1/4 teaspoon ground cumin

24 oz (700 g) lobster claws

3 cups (24 oz/680 g) rice

6 cups (48 fl. oz/1.4 l) chicken broth

1/4 teaspoon saffron

2 chorizo sausages, cooked and cut into chunks

10 uncooked prawns, peeled and deveined

1/2 cup (4 oz/115 g) peas

4 tablespoons capers

Lemon wedges, to garnish

1 Scrub and debeard the mussels and clams, discarding any that do not close when tapped sharply. Set aside.

2 Heat $^1/4$ cup (2 fl. oz/50 ml) of the olive oil in a frying pan. Add the pork, and brown on all sides. Mix in the garlic, onions, tomato, and peppers, stirring constantly until cooked. Set aside.

3 In another pan, heat a further $^1/4$ cup (2 fl. oz/50 ml) olive oil and cook the chicken until browned on all sides. Season with salt, pepper, paprika, rosemary, thyme, and cumin. Transfer the chicken to a plate and set aside.

4 In the same pan, cook the lobster claws over high heat for several minutes until its shell turns pink. Set the pan aside.

5 Preheat the oven to 400 °F (200 °C). Heat 4 tablespoons olive oil in a pan, and sauté the rice until it is translucent. Pour in the chicken broth, and combine well. Add the pork mixture, stirring constantly. Sprinkle in the saffron and continue to stir until well mixed.

6 Transfer the rice into a paella pan. Mix in the lobster, chicken, sausage, clams, mussels, prawns, peas, and capers, combining well. Bake the paella, uncovered, and on the lowest oven shelf, for around 25 minutes, or until all the liquid has been absorbed.

7 Discard any mussels and clams that have failed to open. Serve the paella straight from the pan, garnished with lemon wedges.

PAELLA AL HORNO CON QUESO

Baked Paella with Cheese Topping

A melted cheese topping and creamy rice make this paella an easy family favorite. While water chestnuts are not traditional additions to a paella, their juicy crispness provides the perfect foil for the delicate rice. Serve with warm bread.

SERVES 8 • 15 MINUTES PREPARATION • 75 MINUTES COOKING

$1/4$ cup (2 fl. oz/60 ml) olive oil

32 oz (900 g) skinless, boneless chicken breasts, cut into chunks

$1^1/2$ cups (12 oz/340g) rice

$3^1/4$ cups (26 fl. oz/755 ml) good-quality chicken broth

$1/4$ teaspoon saffron

1 can (11 oz/300 g) cream of celery soup

1 cup (4 oz/115 g) water chestnuts, drained and sliced thin

1 cup (8 fl. oz/230ml) mayonnaise

$1/2$ cup (4 oz/115 g) roasted sweet red peppers, chopped

1 medium yellow onion, chopped

Salt and white pepper, to taste

$1/2$ cup (2 oz/55 g) grated hard cheese (Cheddar or Monterey Jack)

1 Heat the oil in a frying pan over medium heat. Add the chicken and cook until done and browned on all sides.

2 In a separate pan, cook the rice in the chicken broth and saffron for 25 minutes or until the rice is tender and the broth has been absorbed.

3 Pour the rice and chicken into a greased paella pan. Add in the soup, water chestnuts, mayonnaise, red peppers, onion, salt, and pepper. Mix well. Top with grated cheese and bake in the oven at 350 °F (180 °C) for 30 minutes. Serve straight from the oven.

PAELLAS AND ENTRÉES

PAELLA AL CURRY FRÍA

Chilled Paella Curry

This paella recipe demonstrates how the dish may successfully use nontraditional ingredients. Here, the rice is made heavier with the generous use of sour cream and mayonnaise, which in turn provide a creamy balance to the artichokes, mushrooms, and stuffed olives. Chicken breast meat has been added for sustenance, and the dish is infused with the exotic taste of curry. Although this recipe calls for the paella to be served chilled, you may serve it warm if you prefer. The chilled paella, however, makes an excellent picnic lunch.

SERVES 6 • 20 MINUTES PREPARATION • 35 MINUTES COOKING

$3/4$ cup (6 fl. oz/175 ml) olive oil

$1^1/2$ cups (12 oz/340 g) rice

$3^1/4$ cups (26 fl. oz/770 ml) vegetable broth

$1/2$ teaspoon saffron

$1/4$ teaspoon turmeric

16 oz (450 g) skinless, boneless chicken breasts, cut into chunks

1 small green pepper, chopped

1 cup ($2^1/2$ oz/70 g) sliced mushrooms

$1/2$ cup (4 oz/115 g) sliced pimento-stuffed olives

$1/2$ cup (4 fl. oz/120 ml) sour cream

$1/2$ cup (4 fl. oz/120 ml) mayonnaise

2 cups (12 oz/340 g) bottled marinated artichoke hearts, undrained

4 spring onions, sliced

1 tablespoon chopped parsley

$1^1/2$ teaspoons curry powder

1   Heat $1/4$ cup (2 fl. oz/50 ml) of the olive oil in a paella pan. Pour in the rice and sauté for 5 minutes. Add the broth, saffron, and turmeric and cook for 25 minutes or until the rice is tender and the broth has been absorbed. Set aside.

2   While cooking the rice, heat the remaining olive oil in a large frying pan and cook the chicken until done and browned on all sides. Set aside.

3   Add the chicken to the paella pan with the rice, and combine with the remaining ingredients. Refrigerate overnight and serve chilled.

PAELLA DE VENERA Y CHILES VERDES

Scallop Paella with Green Chillies

Roasted sweet red peppers, artichoke hearts, and green chillies lend this paella an interesting array of flavors, and contrast nicely with the mild taste of scallops. This paella can be garnished with lemon wedges, or with additional roasted red peppers arranged in a pattern over the rice.

SERVES 6 • 15 MINUTES PREPARATION • 45 MINUTES COOKING

1/4 **cup (2 fl. oz/60 ml) olive oil**

16 oz (450 g) scallops

1 large onion, chopped

2 cloves garlic, minced

1 1/2 **cups (12 oz/340 g) rice**

3 1/4 **cups (26 fl. oz/770 ml) fish broth**

1/4 **teaspoon saffron**

Salt and pepper, to taste

1 (6 oz/170 g) roasted sweet red pepper, in strips

18 (6 oz/170 g) mild green canned chillies

One 14-ounce (400-g) can artichoke hearts, drained and sprinkled with lemon juice

Lemon wedges (optional), to serve

1 Heat half the olive oil in a paella pan over medium heat. Add the scallops and sauté for 3 minutes. Set the scallops aside and discard the pan juices.

2 Add the remaining olive oil to the pan, and cook the onion and garlic for about 5 minutes over medium heat. Add the rice and cook for a further 5 minutes. Mix in the broth, saffron, salt, and pepper and cook for 10 minutes. Add the roasted red peppers (reserving a few for the garnish, if wished) and the chillies and cook for a further 10 minutes. Add the artichoke hearts and scallops and cook for 5 minutes, or until the broth has been absorbed and the rice is tender.

3 Garnish with lemon wedges or additional roasted sweet red pepper strips, and serve.

TUMBET

Aubergine Casserole

Tumbet, the traditional aubergine dish of the Balearic Islands, can stand on its own as a main course, or can be served as an accompaniment to heartier meat dishes. While many chefs choose to serve tumbet fresh from the oven, this dish is also delectable when left to cool and eaten at room temperature.

SERVES 4 • 80 MINUTES PREPARATION • 45 MINUTES COOKING

3 medium aubergines (eggplants), cut into 1/4-inch (5-mm) slices and sprinkled with salt

1 cup (8 fl. oz/230 ml) olive oil

2 large potatoes, sliced thin

Salt and pepper, to taste

2 small red peppers, chopped

3 small courgettes (zucchini), sliced

3 cloves garlic, minced

2 large tomatoes, skinned, seeded, and chopped

Dash of sugar

1 Leave the aubergine slices in a colander for 1 hour. Blot with paper towels.

2 Heat the olive oil in a pan over low heat. Fry the potato slices until golden. Lay the potato slices along the bottom of a heatproof casserole dish and season with salt and pepper.

3 In the same oil, lightly fry the aubergine slices. Transfer to the casserole and layer the eggplant on top of the potato slices.

4 Fry the peppers in the same oil, transfer to the casserole, and arrange them on top of the aubergine.

5 Fry the zucchini in the same oil. Transfer to the casserole dish and layer over the peppers. Sprinkle with salt and pepper.

6 Fry the garlic cloves in the same pan, adding more oil if necessary, until golden. Mix in the chopped tomatoes, and cook over medium heat for about 20 minutes.

7 Pass the tomato sauce through a sieve, sprinkle with sugar, and pour over the vegetables in the casserole. Transfer to a 350 ° F (180 °C) oven and bake for about 10 minutes. The aubergine casserole can be served hot or at room temperature.

PAELLA DE PICADILLO

Paella with Picadillo

This Andalusian-inspired paella incorporates picadillo, *a light dish served throughout southern Spain during the summer. Traditionally a mixture of oil, peppers, onions, garlic, tomato, and meat (typically chicken or beef), picadillo is widely popular throughout Andalucía and takes only minutes to prepare. Here, picadillo is deliciously paired with paella, creating a more filling main-course meal. This works well as a refreshing lunch or an informal dinner.*

SERVES 6 • 20 MINUTES PREPARATION • 70 MINUTES COOKING

$1/2$ cup ($2^1/2$ oz/70 g) raisins

$1/4$ cup (2 fl. oz/60 ml) dry sherry, warmed

8 oz (225 g) pork sausage

8 oz (225 g) lean ground beef

4 oz (115 g) chorizo sausage

1 medium onion, chopped

3 cloves garlic, minced

One 14-oz (400-g) can diced tomatoes

12 (4 oz/115 g) mild green canned chillies, drained, diced

2 tablespoons sugar

1 teaspoon ground cinnamon

$1/4$ teaspoon ground cumin

$1/8$ teaspoon ground cloves

2 tablespoons olive oil

$1^1/2$ cups (12 oz/340 g) rice

$3^1/4$ cups (26 fl. oz/770 ml) beef broth

$1/4$ teaspoon saffron

1 Add the raisins to the warmed sherry and set aside. Cook the sausage, ground beef, chorizo, onion, and garlic over medium heat until the meat is cooked and browned. Drain the fat. Stir in the raisins and sherry, the undrained tomatoes, the chillies, sugar, cinnamon, cumin, and cloves. Bring to a boil, reduce the heat, and cook, uncovered, for 30 minutes or until almost all the liquid has evaporated, stirring occasionally.

2 Heat the olive oil in a paella pan. Add the rice and sauté for 5 minutes. Pour in the broth and saffron and cook for 20 minutes. Add the sausage mixture, stir, and cook for a further 5 minutes or until the rice is tender and the liquid has been absorbed. Serve immediately.

PAELLA DE POLLO Y TOMATES SECOS

Chicken Paella with Sun-dried Tomatoes

This sophisticated paella is typical of localities such as Madrid, where sun-dried tomatoes are appearing more often in restaurant fare. Here, the dried tomatoes are enhanced by the flavor of dry sherry, and provide a flavorful contrast to the plump rice. Likewise, the interplay of mushrooms, onion, and garlic lends the paella a distinct pungency that is perfectly counterbalanced by the tender chicken. The delicate balance of flavors and simple preparation make this the perfect choice for a paella supper anytime.

SERVES 6 • 40 MINUTES PREPARATION • 55 MINUTES COOKING

1/2 cup (1 oz/28 g) sun-dried tomatoes (not packed in olive oil), chopped

3/4 cup (6 fl. oz/175 ml) dry sherry, for soaking

1/2 cup (4 fl. oz/120 ml) olive oil

24 oz (700 g) skinless, boneless chicken breasts, cut into chunks

1 cup (2 1/2 oz/70 g) sliced mushrooms

1/2 medium onion, chopped fine

3 cloves garlic, chopped fine

3 tablespoons dry sherry

1 1/2 cups (12 oz/300 g) rice

3 1/4 cups (26 fl. oz/770 ml) chicken broth

1/4 teaspoon saffron

1 teaspoon dried basil

1 Soak the chopped sun-dried tomatoes in 3/4 cup (6 fl. oz/175 ml) sherry for 30 minutes, then drain when ready to use.

2 Heat the olive oil in a paella pan over medium heat. Add the chicken and fry until browned on all sides.

3 Meanwhile, in a small saucepan over low heat, cook the mushrooms, onion, and garlic in 3 tablespoons sherry until the mushrooms are tender. Add this mixture to the paella pan and stir well. Mix in the sun-dried tomatoes and cook for 3 minutes. Pour in the rice and cook for a further 5 minutes, stirring frequently. Add the broth, saffron, and basil and cook for about 25 minutes, or until the rice and chicken are tender and the broth has been absorbed. Serve at once.

ZARZUELA

Catalan Fish Stew

The name zarzuela—*literally a light, whimsical operetta—perfectly reflects the bright colors and vibrancy of this unforgettable feast of fish. This dish should be served with warmed, fresh bread to mop up the delicious juices.*

SERVES 6 • 30 MINUTES PREPARATION • 40 MINUTES COOKING

1/2 cup (4 fl. oz/120 ml) olive oil

1 medium yellow onion, peeled and chopped fine

2 cloves garlic, chopped fine

2 medium tomatoes, skinned, seeded, and diced

1 bay leaf

1/4 teaspoon oregano

1/4 teaspoon saffron

8 oz (225 g) monkfish, skinned and cut into chunks

2 cups (16 fl. oz/475 ml) clam juice

1/2 cup (4 fl. oz/120 ml) dry white wine

1 tablespoon chopped parsley

12 clams, scrubbed

12 mussels, scrubbed and debearded

8 oz (225 g) prawns, peeled and deveined

8 oz (225 g) squid, cleaned and sliced into rings

Salt and pepper, to taste

Chopped parsley, to garnish

1 Heat the oil in a large pan and cook the onion and garlic until tender. Add the tomatoes, bay leaf, oregano, and saffron. Cook for about 10 minutes, stirring occasionally. Increase the heat to high and add the monkfish, clam juice, wine, and parsley. Bring to a boil, then add the clams, mussels, prawns, and squid. Reduce the heat to medium, cover and cook for about a further 10 minutes.

2 Discard any mussels and clams that have failed to open. Remove and discard the bay leaf. Season with salt and pepper, transfer to an earthenware serving bowl, and garnish with chopped parsley. Serve immediately, with crusty bread.

Catalan Fish Stew

PAELLA DE CALAMARES

Squid Paella

It is a shame that many tourists in Spain dine on fried squid, with more batter per mouthful than meat, and do not take advantage of the opportunity to savor squid without its bready camouflage. In this paella, the delightful, true flavor of the squid shines through, and is subtly enhanced by the combination of rosemary, cumin, oregano, hot pepper flakes, and sherry.

SERVES 6 • 20 MINUTES PREPARATION • 50 MINUTES COOKING

24 oz (700 g) cleaned squid

Salt and pepper, to taste

1/4 cup (2 fl. oz/50 ml) olive oil

1 large yellow onion, chopped

3 cloves garlic, minced

1 small green pepper, chopped

1 medium tomato, chopped

1 1/4 cups (10 oz/285 g) rice

1/4 cup (2 fl. oz/60 ml) dry sherry

3 1/4 cups (26 fl. oz/770 ml) fish broth

1/4 teaspoon saffron

1/4 **teaspoon dried oregano**

1/4 **teaspoon dried rosemary**

1/4 **teaspoon ground cumin**

1/8 **teaspoon dried hot red pepper flakes**

Lemon wedges, to serve

1 Cut the bodies of the squid into rings, quarter the tentacles, season with salt and pepper, and set aside.

2 Heat the oil in a paella pan over medium heat. Add the onion, garlic, and green pepper and sauté for about 3 minutes. Add the tomato and sauté for a further 3 minutes.

3 Pour in the rice and cook for 5 minutes, stirring constantly. Add the sherry and continue to stir until the sherry evaporates.

4 Add the squid, broth, and the rest of the seasonings and cook for 25 minutes, or until the rice is tender and the broth has been absorbed. Garnish with lemon wedges and serve.

PAELLA DE VERDURAS CON PESTO DE NUECES

Vegetable Paella with Walnut Pesto

The combination of earthy walnut pesto with delicate, saffron-infused rice is simply magical. Chopped walnuts can be sprinkled on top of the paella to further enhance the nutty flavor of the rice.

SERVES 6 • 30 MINUTES PREPARATION • 30 MINUTES COOKING

FOR THE WALNUT PESTO

1 cup (2 oz/55 g) fresh basil leaves, chopped fine

3 tablespoons chopped walnuts

3 tablespoons grated **Manchego** or **Parmesan** cheese

4 cloves garlic, chopped fine

4 tablespoons olive oil

2 tablespoons walnut oil

FOR THE PAELLA

2^1/$_2$ cups (20 fl. oz/600 ml) chicken broth

^{3}/$_4$ cup (6 fl. oz/175 ml) dry white wine

^{1}/$_2$ teaspoon saffron

4 tablespoons olive oil

1 small onion, chopped fine

1 medium red pepper, chopped fine

1^1/$_2$ cups (4 oz/115 g) oyster mushrooms, destemmed and chopped

1^1/$_2$ cups (4 oz/115 g) shiitake mushrooms, destemmed and chopped

2 medium courgettes (zucchini), chopped

2 medium tomatoes, chopped fine

8 artichoke hearts, quartered

2 tablespoons chopped parsley

^{1}/$_2$ teaspoon sweet paprika

1 ^{1}/$_2$ cups (12 oz/340 g) rice

Chopped walnuts, to garnish (optional)

1 First, make the walnut pesto. Place the basil leaves, chopped walnuts, grated cheese, and garlic in a food processor and blend until a paste forms. With the motor still running, add the olive oil and walnut oil little by little, until well incorporated. Set the pesto aside.

2 Combine the chicken broth, white wine, and saffron in a frying pan over low heat. Keep heated until ready for use.

3 To make the paella, heat the olive oil in a paella pan and sauté the onion and pepper over medium heat for several minutes. Mix in the mushrooms, courgettes, tomatoes, artichokes, parsley, and paprika, and cook for several minutes longer.

4 Pour in the rice, and combine well. Stir in the broth mixture and pesto sauce and continue to cook until the liquid has been absorbed and the rice is tender. Serve warm and, if desired, sprinkled with chopped walnuts.

PAELLA VEGETARIANA

Vegetarian Paella

This paella is so moist, full of flavor, and substantial, that you will scarcely notice it is meat-free. The green, red, and yellow peppers add a vibrant splash of color to the pale rice, while the tangy artichoke hearts, delicate peas, and juicy tomatoes ensure that this vegetarian meal will satisfy even the most avid carnivores.

SERVES 6 • 15 MINUTES PREPARATION • 45 MINUTES COOKING

1/4 cup (2 fl. oz/60 ml) olive oil

1 large yellow onion, chopped

5 cloves garlic, minced

4 cups (32 fl. oz/950 ml) vegetable broth

2 cups (16 oz/450 g) rice

1 small red pepper, cut into strips

1 small green pepper, cut into strips

1 small yellow pepper, cut into strips

4 medium tomatoes, seeded and chopped

1 cup (4 oz/115 g) frozen peas, defrosted

2 cups (14 oz/400 g) artichoke hearts, tough outer leaves removed, and quartered

1 lemon

1 Heat the oil in a paella pan and sauté the onion and garlic until the onion is tender and translucent. At the same time, heat the broth in a separate saucepan until simmering.

2 Pour the rice into the paella pan and sauté for about 3 minutes. Add the peppers and tomatoes and cook for a further 3 minutes. Add the simmering vegetable broth and cook over medium heat for 20 minutes or until almost tender and almost all the liquid has been absorbed. Stir in the peas.

3 Sprinkle the artichoke hearts with a few drops of lemon juice and arrange over the rice in an attractive pattern. Continue cooking until the liquid has been absorbed and the rice is tender. Garnish with lemon wedges and serve.

PAELLA DE POLLO, NARANJA Y ALMENDRAS

Chicken and Orange Paella with Almonds

The combination of sweet citrus fruits with meat is attributed to the Moors. Try this delicious pairing of flavors here, in a paella inspired by Valencia. Moorish influences are also present in the generous use of almonds and coriander.

SERVES 6 • 15 MINUTES PREPARATION • 40 MINUTES COOKING

24 oz (700 g) skinless, boneless chicken breasts, cut into chunks

Salt and pepper, to taste

$1/2$ cup (4 fl. oz/120 ml) olive oil

8 cloves garlic, minced

1 medium onion, minced

2 teaspoons grated orange rind

3 cups (24 fl. oz/700 ml) chicken broth

$1/4$ cup (2 fl. oz/60 ml) orange juice

$1/4$ teaspoon saffron

$1^1/2$ cups (12 oz/350 g) rice

1 cup (8 oz/225 g) pimento-stuffed olives, sliced thin

$3/4$ cup ($2^1/2$ oz/75 g) slivered almonds, toasted

1 cup (2 oz/55 g) chopped coriander

Orange wedges, to garnish

1 Generously season the chicken with salt and pepper. Heat the olive oil in a paella pan and sauté the chicken until it is lightly browned on all sides. Add the garlic, onion, and grated orange rind and cook for a further 2 minutes.

2 Meanwhile, heat the chicken broth in a small saucepan. Mix in the orange juice and saffron. Keep warm over low heat until ready for use.

3 Add the rice and olives to the paella pan, combining well. Mix in the broth mixture and allow the rice to cook until the liquid has been absorbed and the rice is tender. Remove from the heat and allow the rice to stand for about 5 minutes, then stir in the toasted sliced almonds and the coriander. Garnish with orange wedges and serve.

PAELLA DE POLLO Y GAMBAS

Chicken and Prawn Paella

An efficient and delicious way to feed a hungry family, this paella relies on condensed soup for its creamy flavor. The chicken and prawns contrast nicely with the sweet red peppers, and the delicately balanced herbs ensure that this paella will become an easy family favorite.

SERVES 8 • 15 MINUTES PREPARATION • 60 MINUTES COOKING

^{1}/2 cup (4 fl. oz/120 ml) olive oil

4 skinless, boneless chicken breasts, cut into small pieces

1 can (about 10 oz/300 g) condensed onion soup

1 can (about 10 oz/300 g) condensed tomato soup

3 cups (24 fl. oz/700 ml) water

5 cloves garlic, minced

1 teaspoon dried oregano

^{1}/2 teaspoon turmeric

^{1}/4 teaspoon dried thyme

Salt and pepper, to taste

2 cups (16 oz/ 450 g) rice

32 oz (900 g) uncooked prawns, peeled and deveined

1 large red pepper, cut into strips

1 large green pepper, cut into strips

1 cup roasted sweet red peppers, chopped

1 cup (8 oz/225 g) stuffed olives, sliced

1 Heat the oil in a paella pan, add the chicken, and cook until browned on all sides. Add the onion and tomato soups, water, garlic, oregano, turmeric, thyme, salt, and pepper and cook, covered, for 15 minutes.

2 Mix in the rice, prawns, peppers, roasted red peppers, and olives and cook, covered, for 25 minutes or until all the liquid has been absorbed, the prawns are cooked, and the chicken and rice are tender. Uncover, allow the paella to cool, and serve.

PAELLA DE BACÓN Y VENERAS

Paella with Bacon and Scallops

Crisp bacon and delicate scallops make
this paella unique. Combined with
saffron-infused rice, this dish is hearty
enough for a filling family supper.

**SERVES 6 • 20 MINUTES PREPARATION •
60 MINUTES COOKING**

8 oz (225 g) bacon

16 oz (450 g) small scallops

1/2 cup (4 fl. oz/125 ml) olive oil

1 medium onion, chopped

3 cloves garlic, minced

1 large green pepper, chopped

**1 large tomato, skinned, seeded, and
chopped**

1 1/2 cups (12 oz/350 g) rice

3 1/4 cups (26 fl. oz/770 ml) fish broth

1/4 teaspoon saffron

3 tablespoons chopped parsley

Salt and pepper, to taste

1 Cook the bacon in a paella pan until
crisp. Set aside and discard all but one
tablespoon of the rendered bacon fat.

2 Add the scallops to the paella pan and
cook until browned, about 5 minutes.
Transfer to a separate bowl (keep
separate from the bacon). Wipe the
paella pan clean.

3 Heat the olive oil in the cleaned paella
pan. Add the onion and cook for about
5 minutes. Add the garlic and the
pepper and cook for about a further
3 minutes. Mix in the tomato and
cook for a further 3 minutes.

4 Pour in the rice and sauté for
5 minutes. Add the fish broth and
saffron, and cook for 20 minutes over
low heat. Add the browned scallops,
bacon, and parsley to the pan and
cook for a further 5 minutes or until
the rice is tender and the broth has
been absorbed. Remove from the
heat, taste for salt and pepper, and
season accordingly. Allow to stand
for 5 minutes before serving.

Paella with Bacon and Scallops

PAELLA DE JAMÓN SERRANO Y ACEITUNAS

Paella with Serrano Ham and Olives

In Spanish tapas bars, serrano ham is often served with a side dish of spiced olives. Try these mutually enhancing flavors here as a savory accompaniment to the spiced, golden rice. Serve with chilled sherry to bring out the ham's delicious saltiness.

SERVES 6 • 15 MINUTES PREPARATION • 50 MINUTES COOKING

1/2 cup (4 fl. oz/125 ml) olive oil

1 small onion, chopped

4 cloves garlic, minced

2 small green peppers, chopped

2 medium tomatoes, skinned, seeded, and chopped

1 1/2 cups (12 oz/350 g) rice

3 1/4 cups (26 fl. oz/770 ml) beef or chicken broth

1/2 teaspoon saffron

1/4 teaspoon dried thyme

1/4 teaspoon ground cumin

Salt and pepper, to taste

8 oz (225 g) serrano ham, julienned

1/2 cup (4 oz/115 g) green Spanish olives, sliced

1 Heat the oil in a paella pan over medium heat. Add the onion and sauté for 5 minutes, or until the onion is soft. Lower the heat, add the garlic and chopped green peppers, and cook for several minutes, until the peppers have softened. Add the tomatoes and sauté for a further 3 minutes.

2 Mix in the rice and allow to cook for a further 5 minutes. Pour in the broth, saffron, thyme, cumin, salt, and pepper and cook for 20 minutes, stirring occasionally. Add the ham and cook for a further 5 minutes or until the rice is tender and the broth has been absorbed. Remove from the heat, sprinkle the sliced olives over the rice, and serve.

PAELLA DE PIMIENTOS ASADOS Y ALCAPARRAS

Roasted Red Pepper Paella with Capers

With its piquant capers, tender prawns, and smoky roasted peppers, this vibrant paella provides a fascinating range of textures and flavors. If wished, sprinkle a few capers over the finished dish before serving.

SERVES 6 • 15 MINUTES PREPARATION • 55 MINUTES COOKING

$1/2$ cup (4 fl. oz/125 ml) olive oil

1 medium onion, chopped

3 cloves garlic, minced

1 large red pepper, seeded and chopped

1 medium tomato, skinned, seeded, and chopped

$1^1/2$ cups (12 oz/340 g) rice

$3^1/4$ cups (26 fl. oz/770 ml) fish broth

16 oz (450 g) uncooked medium prawns, peeled and deveined

$1/4$ teaspoon saffron

$1/4$ teaspoon oregano

1 jar (7) roasted sweet red peppers, drained and sliced

4 tablespoons chopped capers

2 tablespoons chopped parsley

1 Heat the oil in a paella pan over medium heat. Add the onion and cook for 5 minutes. Lower the heat, add the garlic and pepper, and sauté for a further 5 minutes. Stir in the tomato and cook for a further 5 minutes. Pour in the rice and sauté for 7 minutes, stirring.

2 Add the fish broth, prawns, saffron, and oregano and cook for 20 minutes. Mix in the roasted peppers, capers, and parsley and cook for a further 5 minutes or until the rice is tender and the liquid has been absorbed. Serve warm with fresh crusty bread.

PAELLA DE SALCHICHA Y VENERA

Galician Sausage and Scallop Paella

Galicia is famous throughout Spain for the extraordinary quality of its seafood. Due to its exposed position on the northwestern tip of Spain, Galicia has an inordinately large number of fish available to it. In fact, Galician fishermen bring in more scallops each year than anywhere else in Spain. With a nod toward Galicia, this paella teams scallops with prawns and sausage that lend the rice a rich, tender flavor. Enjoy this dish with a chilled glass of Galician wine, such as Albariño.

SERVES 6 TO 8 • 20 MINUTES PREPARATION • 60 MINUTES COOKING

1/4 cup (2 fl. oz/60 ml) olive oil

1 medium yellow onion, chopped

1 large red pepper, chopped

2 cloves garlic, minced

8 oz (225 g) Kielbasa sausage, skinned and chopped

3 cups (24 oz/680 g) rice

6 cups (48 fl. oz/1.4 l) fish broth

1/2 teaspoon saffron

1/2 cup (4 fl. oz/120 ml) dry white wine

8 oz (225 g) scallops

12 oz (350 g) uncooked prawns, peeled and deveined

2 cups (10 oz/280 g) frozen peas, defrosted

3 medium tomatoes, peeled, seeded, and chopped

Salt and white pepper, to taste

1 Heat the olive oil in a paella pan over medium heat. Add the onion and cook for 5 minutes. Throw in the pepper and cook for a further 5 minutes. Add the garlic and continue to cook for about a further 3 minutes. Add the sausage and cook for about 8 minutes, or until done.

2 Mix in the rice and sauté for about a further 5 minutes. Pour in the broth and saffron and cook for a further 15 minutes. Add the wine, scallops, prawns, peas, tomatoes, salt, and pepper. Continue cooking for 8 minutes or until the liquid has been absorbed and the rice is tender. Taste for seasoning, and serve at once.

PAELLA DE ACEITUNAS, ANCHOAS Y TOMATES

Olive, Anchovy, and Tomato Paella

The sharp taste of the anchovies and olives in this paella is balanced by the juicy sweetness of the tomatoes. The result is a flavorful paella with a Mediterranean bite. Capers, too, add a certain piquancy to the rice, and grated Manchego cheese sprinkled on top lends a pleasing richness.

SERVES 6 • 20 MINUTES PREPARATION • 40 MINUTES COOKING

¹/₂ cup (4 fl. oz/120 ml) olive oil

1 medium onion, chopped

3 cloves garlic, minced

1 medium red pepper, chopped

1¹/₂ cups (12 oz/340 g) rice

3¹/₄ cups (26 fl. oz/770 ml) fish broth

¹/₄ teaspoon saffron

5 canned anchovy fillets, packed in olive oil

¹/₄ teaspoon dried hot red pepper flakes

6 medium (24 oz/700 g) fresh tomatoes, skinned, seeded, and chopped

¹/₃ cup (2¹/₂ oz/70 g) pimento-stuffed olives, chopped

4 tablespoons capers, drained

Salt and pepper, to taste

Grated Manchego or Parmesan cheese, to taste

1 Heat the olive oil in a paella pan, add the onion, and sauté for about 5 minutes or until the onion softens. Add the garlic and pepper and sauté for several minutes, until the pepper softens. Mix in the rice and allow to cook for 5 minutes. Pour in the broth and saffron, and cook for about 20 minutes.

2 Meanwhile, while the rice is cooking, mash the anchovies and pepper flakes together in a mortar. In a separate bowl, mix together the tomatoes, olives, and capers. Add the anchovy paste, with salt and pepper to taste, to the tomato mixture and combine thoroughly.

3 Add this mixture to the rice, combine well, and allow the rice to cook for a further 5 minutes. Sprinkle some grated Manchego cheese over the rice, and serve.

PAELLA DE POLLO, SALCHICHA Y CHAMPIÑONES

Chicken and Sausage Paella with Mushrooms

This mixed sausage and chicken paella is suitable for either an elegant lunch or an informal, filling supper. For extra flavor, use spicy pork sausage and garnish with capers.

SERVES 6 • 15 MINUTES PREPARATION • 50 MINUTES COOKING

$1/2$ cup (4 fl. oz/120 ml) olive oil

16 oz (450 g) skinless, boneless chicken breasts, cut into pieces

16 oz (450 g) pork sausage

1 medium (5 oz/140 g) onion, chopped

2 cloves garlic, chopped

2 medium green peppers, chopped

5 cups (12 oz/340 g) mushrooms, sliced

1 large tomato, skinned, seeded, and chopped

$1^{1}/2$ cups (12 oz/340 g) rice

$3^{1}/4$ cups (26 fl. oz/770 ml) chicken broth

$1/2$ teaspoon saffron

$1/4$ teaspoon ground cumin

Salt and pepper, to taste

2 to 3 tablespoons capers, to garnish (optional)

1 Heat the oil in a paella pan over medium heat. Add the chicken and cook until browned on all sides. Transfer the chicken to a dish and set aside.

2 Add the sausage to the paella pan and cook until done. Transfer to the plate with the chicken.

3 Add the onion to the paella pan and sauté for 5 minutes or until tender. Lower the heat, add the garlic, and sauté for about 2 minutes. Add the green peppers, mushrooms, and chopped tomato and cook until the peppers and mushrooms have softened.

4 Mix in the rice and sauté for 5 minutes. Add the chicken broth, chicken, sausage, saffron, cumin, salt, and pepper and cook over medium heat until the chicken and rice are tender and all the broth has been absorbed. Allow to cool for about 5 minutes before serving. If desired, garnish with capers.

TORTILLA DE ESPÁRRAGOS

Asparagus Omelette

Although this unique omelette is usually served hot straight from the skillet, it is also delicious served cold or at room temperature. Indeed, cooled leftovers of this delectable dish with a glass of amontillado sherry make for a perfect picnic lunch. While some slice this omelette into bite-size squares and serve it as a tapa, it is more common to see this dish served in more generous portions for lunch or a light supper.

SERVES 4 • 15 MINUTES PREPARATION • 40 MINUTES COOKING

1/2 regular bunch (8 oz/225 g) asparagus

2 cups (16 fl. oz/475 ml) water

2 tablespoons water

2 tablespoons olive oil

1 medium onion, chopped

1 clove garlic, chopped fine

Pinch of salt

Pinch of pepper

1/3 cup (1 oz/28 g) grated Manchego cheese

8 medium eggs, beaten

Lemon juice

1 tomato, sliced, to garnish

1 Wash the asparagus and trim it into 1-inch (2.5-cm) pieces. Bring water to a boil in a saucepan and add the asparagus pieces. Cook for about 2 to 3 minutes or until tender. Drain the asparagus and set aside.

2 Heat the olive oil over low heat in a 12-inch (30-cm) pan. Add the chopped onion and garlic and cook until tender. Stir in the asparagus, salt, pepper, and grated cheese.

3 Reduce the heat to low and pour the beaten eggs into the pan. Do not stir the mixture. Cook, covered, until the omelette sets, around 15 to 20 minutes. Slice into four portions and sprinkle with lemon juice.

4 Garnish with sliced tomato and serve.

Asparagus Omelette

PAELLA FÁCIL Y RÁPIDA DE POLLO

Quick and Easy Chicken Paella

A substantial, versatile paella that provides a protein-packed meal with a sunny Mediterranean flavor. If desired, pine nuts can be sprinkled over the cooked rice for a crisp garnish.

SERVES 6 • 10 MINUTES PREPARATION • 45 MINUTES COOKING

$^1/_4$ cup (2 fl. oz/60 ml) olive oil

48 oz (1.3 kg) skinless, boneless chicken breasts, cut into small chunks

1 medium onion, chopped

3 cloves garlic, minced

One 14-oz (400-g) can tomatoes, diced

$^1/_2$ teaspoon saffron

3$^1/_4$ cups (26 fl. oz/770 ml) chicken broth

1 bay leaf

1 $^1/_2$ cups (12 oz/340 g) rice

Salt and pepper, to taste

3 cups (15 oz/425 g) frozen peas, defrosted

$^1/_2$ cup (4 oz/115 g) pimento-stuffed olives, sliced thin

1 Heat the oil in a paella pan over medium heat. Add the chicken pieces and fry until browned. Add the onion and garlic and sauté for about 5 minutes.

2 Mix in the tomatoes, saffron, chicken broth, and bay leaf and cook over low heat for about 10 minutes.

3 Add the rice, salt, and pepper and cook for 15 minutes.

4 Stir in the peas and olives and cook until the chicken and rice are tender and the broth has been absorbed. Remove the bay leaf before serving.

PAELLA GRIEGA

Greek Paella with Smoked Salmon and Crumbled Feta Cheese

Inspired by the cuisine of Greece, this paella combines olives, crumbled feta cheese, smoked salmon, and dill with Spain's saffron-enhanced rice. The result is a perfect fusion of the sunny flavors of the Mediterranean.

SERVES 6 • 10 MINUTES PREPARATION • 40 MINUTES COOKING

$^1/_4$ **cup (2 fl. oz/60 ml) olive oil**

3 cloves garlic, chopped

1 large onion, minced

1 small green pepper, chopped

1 large tomato, skinned, seeded, and diced

1$^1/_2$ cups (12 oz/350 g) rice

3$^1/_4$ cups (26 fl. oz/770 ml) chicken broth

1 teaspoon dried dill

$^1/_4$ **teaspoon saffron**

Dash of cayenne pepper

6 oz (175 g) smoked salmon, cut into thin strips

$^1/_2$ **cup (4 oz/115 g) crumbled feta cheese**

1 Heat the oil in a paella pan over medium heat. Add the garlic, onion, and green pepper and sauté for about 3 minutes, or until softened. Add the tomato and cook for a further 3 minutes.

2 Mix in the rice and sauté, stirring, for several minutes. Add the broth, dill, saffron, and cayenne pepper, bring to a boil, and cook for 20 minutes. Add the smoked salmon and cook for a further 5 minutes or until the rice is tender and the liquid has been absorbed. Stir in the feta cheese and serve.

PAELLA DE PESCADO

Classic Seafood Paella

A paella staple popular throughout all of Spain, this recipe is a feast for the eyes as well as the stomach. This paella adheres to the Valencian preference of not mixing seafood with poultry or red meat. Fresh squid, clams, mussels, prawns, and monkfish combine beautifully with the assertive flavor of the rice.

SERVES 6 TO 8 • 30 MINUTES PREPARATION • 60 MINUTES COOKING

8 oz (225 g) mussels

8 oz (225 g) clams

5 tablespoons olive oil

8 oz (225 g) monkfish, quartered

8 oz (225 g) squid, cleaned and cut into strips

2 small onions, chopped

5 cloves garlic, minced

1 small green pepper, diced

1 small red pepper, diced

3 large ripe tomatoes, skinned, seeded, and chopped

2 cups (16 oz/450 g) rice

4 cups (32 fl. oz/940 ml) fish broth

$1/2$ teaspoon powdered saffron

Salt and pepper, to taste

8 oz (225 g) uncooked large prawns, peeled and deveined

1 Scrub the mussels and clams thoroughly, removing all beards and barnacles. Discard any that fail to close when tapped sharply. Set the mussels and clams aside.

2 Heat 4 tablespoons olive oil in a paella pan over medium heat. Add the monkfish and squid and cook for 7 to 8 minutes. Transfer to another pan.

3 Add the remaining tablespoon of olive oil to the paella pan and cook the onions and garlic until the onions are tender. Add the peppers and cook for about 5 minutes. Mix in the tomatoes and continue to cook for a further 8 to 10 minutes.

4 Add the monkfish, squid, and rice to the paella pan. Cook, stirring frequently, for 5 minutes. Stir in the fish broth, saffron, salt, and pepper, and allow to simmer for 5 minutes. Add the prawns, mussels, and clams and continue to cook over low heat until all the liquid has been absorbed, about 20 minutes. Discard any mussels and clams that have failed to open. Serve at once.

PAELLA DE GAMBAS CON CURRY

Curried Prawn Paella

Inspired by Thai cuisine, this unusual paella combines the best of East and West. To ensure a harmonious mix of flavors, this recipe uses paprika instead of saffron to imbue the rice with its traditional golden hue. The addition of coconut milk, lemon grass, and red curry paste lends this rice dish an exotic and flavorful accent. If you wish to make this dish even spicier, add an extra teaspoon of red curry paste.

SERVES 6 • 20 MINUTES PREPARATION • 35 MINUTES COOKING

4 tablespoons olive oil

1 medium onion, minced

3 teaspoons Thai red curry paste

16 oz (450 g) uncooked medium prawns, peeled and deveined

2 medium red peppers, cut into long, thin strips

2 medium carrots, sliced thin crosswise

1¹/₂ cups (12 oz/350 g) rice

1¹/₂ cups (12 fl. oz/350 ml) fish broth

One 14-oz (400-ml) can unsweetened coconut milk

1 tablespoon dried lemon grass

¹/₂ teaspoon paprika

3 tablespoons chopped coriander

1 Heat the oil in a paella pan over medium heat. Add the onion and sauté for about 5 minutes or until golden. Add the curry paste and prawns and cook over high heat for 1 to 2 minutes, or until the prawns turn pink.

2 Reduce the heat to medium, add the peppers and carrots, and sauté for several minutes. Mix in the rice, fish broth, coconut milk, lemon grass, and paprika and reduce the heat to low. Cook until the liquid has been absorbed and the rice is tender. When the rice is ready, remove the pan from heat, mix in the coriander, and serve.

PAELLA DE ANCHOAS CON ALMENDRAS Y ALCAPARRAS

Anchovy Paella with Almonds and Capers

This piquant version of paella relies on traditional Mediterranean ingredients for its robust flavor. While the ingredients used are not subtle, they combine harmoniously into a savory paella of unusual texture.

SERVES 6 • 10 MINUTES PREPARATION • 35 MINUTES COOKING

3 cups (24 fl. oz/700 ml) vegetable broth

1/4 cup (2 fl. oz/60 ml) dry white wine

1/2 teaspoon saffron

1/4 cup (2 fl. oz/50 ml) olive oil

5 tablespoons slivered almonds

1 large onion, chopped fine

8 cloves garlic, minced

1 red chilli, chopped

1 medium green pepper, chopped

1/2 cup (4 oz/115 g) pimento-stuffed olives, sliced thin

1/4 cup (2 oz/50 g) capers

10 canned anchovy fillets, packed in olive oil, chopped

3 tablespoons chopped parsley

1/2 cup (1 1/2 oz/42 g) grated Manchego or Parmesan cheese

1 1/2 cups (12 oz/340 g) rice

Lemon wedges, to garnish

1 Heat the vegetable broth in a pan over low heat. Add the wine and saffron and keep over low heat until ready for use.

2 Heat the olive oil in a paella pan, add the almonds, and fry for 1 to 2 minutes. Add the onion and garlic and sauté for about 5 minutes or until they are soft. Mix in the chilli and pepper, and sauté for a further 2 to 3 minutes.

3 Stir in the olives, capers, anchovy fillets, parsley, and cheese. Add the rice and combine well. Pour in the vegetable broth mixture and continue to stir. Sauté until all the liquid has been absorbed and the rice is tender. Garnish with lemon wedges and serve.

PAELLA ESMERALDA

Emerald Paella

Based on Cataluña's spinach with raisins and pine nuts (page 32), this vegetable paella owes its name to the generous use of peppers, parsley, olives, and spinach that flavor the rice. This paella can include raisins, if you like. Although not a traditional accompaniment to paella, they can add an unexpected and welcome sweetness to the saffron-enhanced rice.

SERVES 6 • 15 MINUTES PREPARATION • 40 MINUTES COOKING

$3^1/4$ cups (26 fl. oz/770 ml) vegetable broth

$1^1/2$ tablespoons chopped parsley

1 teaspoon dried basil

$1/2$ teaspoon saffron

$1/4$ teaspoon ground cumin

6 tablespoons olive oil

4 tablespoons pine nuts

1 large onion, chopped fine

8 cloves garlic, minced

1 medium green pepper, chopped fine

$3/4$ cup (6 oz/170 g) pimento-stuffed olives, chopped

5 cups (10 oz/280 g) spinach leaves, destemmed and chopped

$1^1/2$ cups (12 oz/340 g) rice

$1/2$ cup ($1^1/2$ oz/42 g) grated Manchego or Parmesan cheese

1 Combine the vegetable broth, parsley, basil, saffron, and cumin in a pan and heat over low heat. Set aside.

2 Heat the olive oil in the paella pan and lightly toast the pine nuts. Add the onion, garlic, and pepper and sauté until tender. Add the olives and the spinach and cook for several minutes, until the spinach has wilted.

3 Mix in the rice and pour in the warm vegetable broth, combining well. Cook until the rice is tender and all the broth has been absorbed, about 25 minutes. Mix in the cheese, and allow to cool for several minutes before serving.

Emerald Paella

PAELLA DE ALMEJAS, MEJILLONES Y GAMBAS

Paella with Clams, Mussels, and Prawns

This delightful array of prawns, mussels, and clams is a seafood lover's dream. With a touch of sherry and pimento-stuffed olives added to the mix, this rice evokes the taste of Andalucía in the summer. Be sure to discard any mussels or clams that fail to close when tapped sharply before you begin cooking.

SERVES 6 • 15 MINUTES PREPARATION • 45 MINUTES COOKING

1/4 cup (2 fl. oz/60 ml) olive oil

1 large onion, chopped

4 cloves garlic, minced

1 large green pepper, chopped

1 large tomato, chopped

1 1/2 cups (12 oz/350 g) rice

1/4 cup (2 fl. oz/50 ml) dry sherry

32 oz (900 g) mussels, scrubbed and debearded

16 oz (450 g) clams, scrubbed

3 1/4 cups (26 fl. oz/770 ml) fish broth

1/4 teaspoon saffron

8oz (225 g) uncooked medium prawns, peeled and deveined

1/4 cup (2 oz/55 g) pimento-stuffed olives, chopped

1 Heat the oil in a paella pan over medium heat. Add the onion, garlic, and green pepper and sauté for about 3 to 5 minutes. Add the chopped tomato and cook for a further 3 minutes. Pour in the rice and cook, stirring frequently, for several minutes. Mix in the sherry and cook for 3 minutes, or until evaporated.

2 Add the mussels, clams, broth, and saffron and cook for about 10 minutes. Add the prawns and olives and cook for about 15 minutes, or until all the broth has been absorbed, the prawns are cooked, the rice is tender, and the mussels and clams are open. Discard any mussels or clams that have failed to open before you serve the paella.

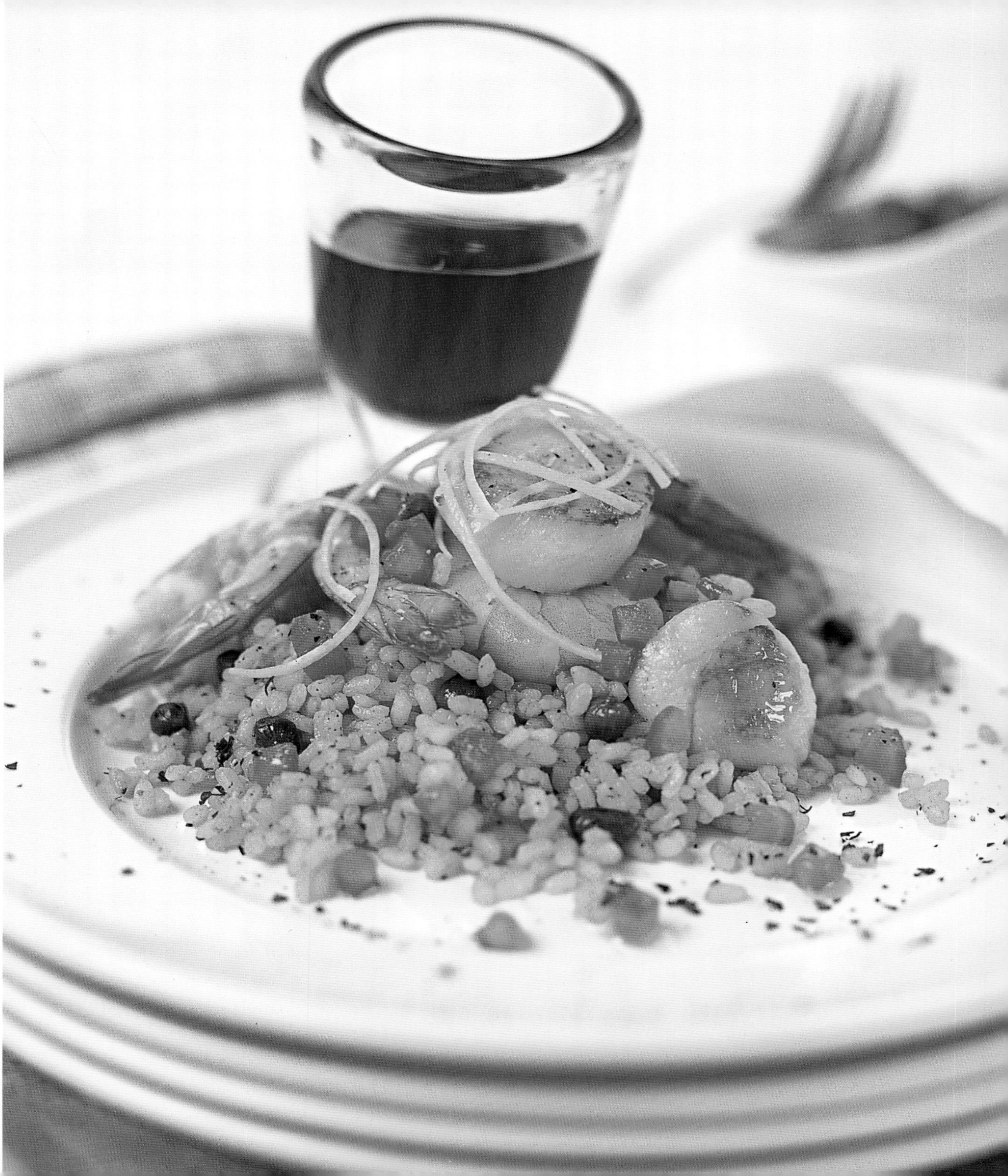

PAELLA DE GAMBAS, AJO Y LIMÓN

Lemon, Prawn, and Garlic Paella

This simple paella recipe relies on the delicate flavors of prawns and scallop to infuse the rice with the subtle, yet distinct, taste of the ocean. Tomatoes and capers add a pleasing splash of color to this dish. Enjoy this paella with chilled sherry, which brings out the sweetness of the scallops and prawns.

SERVES 6 • 20 MINUTES PREPARATION • 40 MINUTES COOKING

$1/4$ **cup (2 fl. oz/60 ml) olive oil**

5 cloves garlic, minced

2 large, ripe tomatoes, skinned, seeded, and chopped

$1^1/2$ **cups (12 oz/340 g) rice**

16 oz (450 g) uncooked medium prawns, peeled and deveined

$3^1/4$ **cups (26 fl. oz/770 ml) fish broth**

$1/4$ **teaspoon saffron**

Salt and pepper, to taste

8 oz (225 g) scallops

3 tablespoons capers

Juice of $1/2$ lemon

1 teaspoon grated lemon rind

3 tablespoons chopped parsley

1 Heat the oil over medium heat in a paella pan. Add the minced garlic and cook, stirring frequently, for 2 minutes. Add the tomatoes and cook for a further 5 minutes. Stir in the rice and sauté for a further 5 minutes. Add the prawns, broth, saffron, salt, and pepper, and cook for a further 15 minutes.

2 Mix in the scallops and capers and sauté for a further 10 minutes, or until the rice is tender and all the broth has been absorbed. Remove from the heat and add the lemon juice, rind, and parsley. Serve warm, straight from the pan.

PAELLA ROJA

Red Paella

This colorful paella gets its name from the addition of paprika and red peppers, which flavor the rice. The sweetness of the roasted sweet red peppers in this recipe is the perfect counterpoint to the saltiness of the clams and aromatic pungency of the garlic. Filling but light, this paella leaves ample room for a creamy Spanish dessert.

SERVES 8 • 15 MINUTES PREPARATION • 50 MINUTES COOKING

$3/4$ cup (6 fl. oz/175 ml) olive oil

1 medium onion, chopped

2 medium red peppers, chopped

3 cloves garlic, minced

3 cups (24 oz/680 g) rice

8 oz (225 g) clams, scrubbed

12 oz (350 g) uncooked prawns, peeled and deveined

$6^{1}/4$ cups (50 fl. oz/1.5 l) fish or chicken broth

$1/2$ teaspoon Spanish paprika

$1/2$ teaspoon saffron

Salt and pepper, to taste

1 cup (4 fl. oz/115 g) sliced roasted sweet red peppers, canned or homemade

1 Heat the olive oil over medium heat in a paella pan. Add the onion and red pepper and cook until the onion begins to soften. Add the garlic and cook for a further 5 minutes. Pour in the rice and cook, stirring constantly, for a further 5 minutes or until the rice is translucent. Mix in the clams, prawns, broth, paprika, saffron, salt, and pepper. Cover and cook for 25 minutes or until all the liquid has been absorbed.

2 Remove from the heat. Taste for salt, and arrange the sweet red peppers in a pattern over the rice. Cover again and wait 5 minutes before serving.

PAELLA DE GAMBAS, JAMÓN Y CHORIZO

Sweet Prawn Paella with Ham and Sausage

This mixed paella is touched with a hint of sweetness provided by the unexpected addition of sugar and soy sauce. This sweet and salty combination, reminiscent of the Moors, works amazingly well in a rice dish.

SERVES 8 • 20 MINUTES PREPARATION • 40 MINUTES COOKING

1/2 cup (4 fl. oz/50 ml) olive oil

6 oz (175 g) chorizo sausage, sliced

1 large onion, chopped

5 cloves garlic, minced

2 small green peppers, diced

4 cups (32 fl. oz/950 ml) chicken broth

One 14-oz (400-g) can plum tomatoes, drained and chopped

2 tablespoons chopped parsley

1 tablespoon sugar

1 tablespoon soy sauce

1 teaspoon salt

1 teaspoon turmeric

1/2 teaspoon saffron

1/4 teaspoon dried oregano

1/4 teaspoon black pepper

1 bay leaf

2 cups (24 oz/680 g) rice

16 oz (450 g) small prawns

2 cups (12 oz/340 g) diced cooked ham

1 Heat the olive oil in a paella pan over medium heat. Add the chorizo sausage, onion, and garlic and sauté until the onions are soft. Stir in the peppers, broth, tomatoes, parsley, sugar, soy sauce, salt, turmeric, saffron, oregano, pepper, and bay leaf, and cook for 10 minutes.

2 Add the rice and cook for a further 10 minutes. Add the prawns and ham, cover, and cook until all the liquid has been absorbed, about 10 more minutes. Discard the bay leaf before serving.

PAELLA DE ALCACHOFAS Y JAMÓN

Artichoke and Ham Paella

Smoked ham, savory artichokes, and a cheese-flavored rice make this simple paella an easy choice for supper. Mushrooms can also be added to lend the rice an earthy flavor.

SERVES 6 • 10 MINUTES PREPARATION • 40 MINUTES COOKING

1/4 cup (2 fl. oz/60 ml) olive oil

1 small onion, chopped

3 cloves garlic, minced

1 1/2 cups (12 oz/340 g) rice

3 1/4 cups (26 fl. oz/770 ml) chicken broth

1/2 teaspoon saffron

One 14-oz (400-g) can artichoke hearts, quartered and sprinkled with lemon juice

1 cup (115 g) diced smoked ham

1/2 cup (1 1/2 oz/42 g) grated **Manchego** or **Parmesan cheese**

2 tablespoons chopped parsley

1 Heat the olive oil in a paella pan. Add the onion and garlic and cook over low heat for 5 minutes. Add the rice and sauté for 5 minutes. Add the broth and saffron and cook for a further 20 minutes. Mix in the artichoke hearts and ham and cook for a further 5 minutes, or until the rice is tender and all the broth has been absorbed.

2 Remove from the heat, sprinkle with cheese and parsley, and serve.

PAELLA VERDE

Green Paella

Paella Verde is inspired by a paella served in Alicante, a vibrant Valencian city on the Mediterranean coast known for the quality of its clams. This paella gets its colorful name from the peppers, parsley, and a host of green vegetables that are used to flavor the dish. If an extra splash of green is desired, feel free to add broccoli florets.

SERVES 8 • 15 MINUTES PREPARATION • 55 MINUTES COOKING

1/2 cup (4 fl. oz/125 ml) olive oil

16 oz (450 g) lean pork, diced

1 large onion, chopped

2 large green peppers, chopped

1 medium tomato, skinned and diced

4 cloves garlic, minced

3 cups (24 oz/680 g) rice

24 oz (700 g) clams, scrubbed

6 1/4 cups (50 fl. oz/1.5 l) good-quality fish or chicken broth

1 1/2 cups (6 oz/170 g) frozen green peas, defrosted

1 cup (4 oz/115 g) frozen green beans, defrosted

One 14-oz (400-g) can artichoke hearts

1 cup (5 1/2 oz/150 g) frozen asparagus, defrosted

1/4 teaspoon saffron

1/2 cup (3 1/2 oz/100 g) chopped flat-leaf parsley

Salt and pepper, to taste

1 Heat half the olive oil in a paella pan. Add the pork and cook until browned on all sides. Set aside.

2 Wipe the pan clean and heat the remaining oil. Add the onion and green peppers. When the onion begins to soften, add the tomato and garlic and cook for a further 5 minutes.

3 Pour in the rice and cook, stirring constantly, for 5 minutes or until the rice is translucent. Mix in the pork, clams, broth, vegetables, and saffron and cook for 20 minutes. Add the parsley, salt, and pepper and cook for a further 5 minutes, or until all the liquid has been absorbed. Allow to stand for 5 minutes before serving, to ensure the absorption of all the flavors.

Green Paella

PAELLA MIXTA RÁPIDA

Quick Mixed Paella

Laced with chicken and prawns and studded with sausage, this paella will tempt the fussiest of palates. Fewer vegetables and accompaniments allow the flavor of the tender meat in this paella to shine through.

SERVES 8 • 10 MINUTES PREPARATION • 60 MINUTES COOKING

8 oz (225 g) chorizo or Italian sausage, cut into small pieces

1/4 cup (2 fl. oz/60 ml) olive oil

1 small onion, chopped

1 medium red pepper, chopped

1 medium green pepper, chopped

3 cloves garlic, minced

3 skinless, boneless chicken breasts, cut into small pieces

2 1/2 cups (20 oz/560 g) rice

5 cups (40 fl. oz/1.2 l) chicken, fish, or vegetable broth

Salt and pepper, to taste

16 oz (450 g) uncooked prawns, peeled and deveined

2 large tomatoes, skinned, seeded, and chopped

1/4 teaspoon saffron

1   Sauté the chorizo or Italian sausage in a paella pan over medium-high heat until cooked. Reduce heat and add the olive oil, onion, peppers, and garlic and cook for 5 minutes or until the onion is soft. Add the chicken and cook until browned on all sides.

2   Mix in the rice and sauté for 5 minutes or until translucent. Pour in the broth, add salt and pepper, and bring to a boil. Reduce the heat and simmer, covered, for about 20 minutes or until most of the liquid has been absorbed.

3   Uncover, stir the mixture, and add the prawns, tomatoes, and saffron. Cook until the rice is tender, the liquid has been absorbed, and the prawns are cooked and have turned pink. Serve straight from the pan.

PAELLA DE CHAMPIÑONES

Mixed Mushroom Paella

Three varieties of mushrooms lend this paella its distinctive taste and texture. Butter and Manchego cheese impart a creamy richness to the earthy rice, while the sherry, thyme, and basil add flavor and interest to the dish.

SERVES 6 • 15 MINUTES PREPARATION • 30 MINUTES COOKING

2 tablespoons olive oil

2 medium onions, chopped fine

6 cloves garlic, minced

1 cup (4 oz/115 g) diced serrano ham or prosciutto

1 cup (4 oz/115 g) shiitake mushrooms, stemmed and chopped

1 cup (4 oz/115 g) crimini mushrooms, stemmed and chopped

1 cup (4 oz/115 g) oyster mushrooms, stemmed and chopped

1$\frac{1}{2}$ cups (12 oz/350 g) rice

2$\frac{3}{4}$ cups (22 fl. oz/650 ml) chicken broth

1/2 cup (4 fl. oz/120 ml) sherry

$\frac{1}{2}$ teaspoon saffron

1 cup (3 oz/85 g) grated **Manchego** or **Parmesan** cheese

$\frac{1}{4}$ stick (1 oz/25 g) butter, softened

2 tablespoons chopped fresh basil leaves

1 tablespoon chopped fresh thyme

Salt and pepper, to taste

1 Heat the oil in a paella pan over medium heat. Add the onion and garlic and sauté for about 5 minutes or until tender. Add the ham and mushrooms, and sauté for a further several minutes, until the mushrooms have softened.

2 Pour in the rice, and combine well with the ingredients in the pan. Add the broth, sherry, and saffron. Simmer, stirring occasionally, until the liquid has almost been absorbed and the mixture is creamy. Stir in the Manchego or Parmesan cheese, butter, basil, and thyme. Remove from the heat, and allow the paella to cool for 5 minutes. Season with salt and pepper to taste, and serve.

PAELLA EXPRÉS

Express Paella

Another recipe that uses a nontraditional paella method—the pressure cooker—to produce a meal quickly in an emergency. The guests that "just happened to drop by" will never guess that this flavorful paella was prepared in under 15 minutes! Although not as elaborate as some of its more traditionally prepared cousins, this paella nevertheless yields surprisingly good returns for the scant effort invested, and is a perfect choice for when you are simply too tired or busy to cook.

SERVES 6 • 15 MINUTES PREPARATION • 30 MINUTES COOKING

1 small onion, diced

1 medium green pepper, diced

$1/4$ cup (2 fl. oz/60 ml) olive oil

1 large tomato, skinned and diced

$1^1/2$ cups (12 oz/340 g) rice

$3^1/4$ cups (26 fl. oz/770 ml) chicken broth

8 oz (225 g) uncooked medium prawns, peeled and deveined

$1/4$ teaspoon saffron

$1/4$ teaspoon ground cumin

Freshly ground black pepper, to taste

Lemon wedges, to garnish

1 In a pressure cooker, sauté the onion and pepper in the olive oil until the onion is tender. Add the tomato and cook for a further 5 minutes. Add the rice and sauté until translucent. Pour in the broth, prawns, saffron, cumin, and pepper, close the pressure cooker, bring to high pressure over medium heat, and cook for a further 3 minutes.

2 Transfer to a paella pan or serving platter, garnish with lemon wedges, and serve.

PAELLA EXTREMEÑA

Hearty Extremadura Paella

Although critics have dismissed the cuisine of Spain's arid Extremadura region as mere "country cooking," it is slowly gaining popularity among those who appreciate basic, unadorned fare. Relying primarily on pork, ham, lamb, and potatoes, recipes from Extremadura tend to be simple, yet immensely satisfying. This very filling paella, influenced by Extremaduran cuisine, features generous portions of serrano ham, pork loin, chicken, and chorizo (the delectable Spanish sausage which, some speculate, originated in Extremadura).

SERVES 8 • 20 MINUTES PREPARATION • 80 MINUTES COOKING

$3/4$ cup (6 fl. oz/175 ml) olive oil

8 oz (225 g) pork loin, cleaned and diced

8 oz (225 g) skinless, boneless chicken breasts, diced

2 medium onions, chopped

5 cloves garlic, minced

8 oz (225 g) chorizo sausage, case removed and crumbled or sliced

2 medium green peppers, cut into thin strips

2 large ripe tomatoes, skinned, seeded, and chopped

2 cups (16 oz/450 g) rice

$4^1/4$ cups (34 fl. oz/1 l) beef broth

1 teaspoon turmeric

$1/4$ teaspoon saffron

$1/4$ teaspoon dried oregano

Pinch of dried thyme

Salt and freshly ground pepper, to taste

8 oz (225 g) serrano ham, chopped

1 Heat half of the olive oil in a paella pan over medium heat. Add the pork and cook until done, about 10 minutes. Transfer to a different pan and set aside.

2 Cook the chicken in the paella pan until done, about 10 minutes. Transfer the chicken to the pan containing the pork.

3 Pour the remaining oil in the paella pan and sauté the onions for 5 minutes. Add the garlic and cook for a further 3 minutes. Add the chorizo sausage and cook for 5 minutes. Stir in the peppers and tomatoes and cook for a further 10 minutes over low heat.

4 Increase the heat to medium, add the rice to the pan, and sauté for 5 minutes. Pour in the broth. Mix in the cooked pork and chicken, and add the turmeric, saffron, oregano, thyme, salt, and pepper. Cook for 15 minutes. Add the ham and cook for a further 7 minutes or until the liquid has been absorbed and the rice is tender.

RAPE CON LIMÓN

Lemon-flavored Monkfish

It would be difficult to imagine life on the Iberian Peninsula without lemons. Fresh lemons, and their juice, are praised by the Spanish for both their flavor and supposed medicinal qualities. These tangy fruits lend a distinctive, zesty touch to many Spanish dishes, as evidenced in this dish, which uses the lemon's tartness to enhance this delicate, mild-tasting fish.

SERVES 4 • 10 MINUTES PREPARATION • 15 MINUTES COOKING

1 cup (8 fl. oz/230 ml) dry white wine

Grated rind of 1 small lemon

Juice of 1 small lemon

2 cloves garlic, minced

Salt and freshly ground white pepper

3 tablespoons olive oil

Four 6-oz (175-g) slices monkfish

3 tablespoons capers

1 In a food processor or blender, combine the wine, lemon rind, lemon juice, garlic, salt, and pepper until a smooth sauce is formed. Set aside.

2 Pour the olive oil into a pan and fry the monkfish over medium heat until golden brown all over. Reduce the heat and cover the fish with the wine sauce. Allow to simmer for several minutes, then add in the capers. Transfer to an attractive platter and serve immediately.

PAELLA CON QUESO Y ALMEJAS

Easy Paella with Cheddar Cheese and Clams

An impossibly easy recipe that will make paella traditionalists bluster with indignation. Unorthodox? Perhaps. But in the real world, company drops by when you least expect it. Armed with this recipe, you can bake a delicious paella for unexpected guests while tidying up and serving drinks.

SERVES 6 • 10 MINUTES PREPARATION • 75 MINUTES COOKING

1 cup (8 oz/225 g) uncooked rice

1 10-oz (300-g) can Cheddar cheese soup

1 soup can water

1 small onion, chopped

Three 14-oz (400-g) cans baby clams

1 small red pepper, chopped

$1/2$ celery stalk, chopped

1 teaspoon salt

$1/4$ teaspoon dried hot red pepper flakes

1 Preheat the oven to 350 °F (180 °C). Mix all the ingredients together in a paella pan and cover with foil. Bake for $1^1/4$ hours, stirring lightly once during cooking.

2 Uncover the foil and serve warm straight from the pan.

HELADO DE CANELA

Cinnamon Ice Cream

Ice cream in Spain is rarely served as a dessert at home. Rather, it is a decadent treat found at sidewalk cafés and in restaurants. Likewise, ice cream stands are a common sight around Spain in the summer, especially throughout beach towns. Recreate the feeling of a languorous afternoon at the café with this cinnamon-flavored ice cream. Delicious yet light, it is easy to see why this is a Spanish summertime favorite.

SERVES 4 • 30 MINUTES PREPARATION PLUS CHILLING TIME • 15 MINUTES COOKING

4 cups (30 fl. oz/900 ml) milk

1 cinnamon stick, about 4 inches (10 cm) long

1 strip lemon rind, about 3 to 4 inches (7.5 to 10 cm) long

6 medium egg yolks

1^1/$_2$ cups (10^1/$_2$ oz/300 g) sugar

Sprigs of fresh mint, to decorate

1 In a medium saucepan, heat 2 cups (15 fl. oz/450 ml) of the milk with the cinnamon stick and lemon rind. Allow to simmer gently, then remove from heat and set aside.

2 In a separate bowl, beat the egg yolks well. Add the remaining milk and sugar, combining thoroughly.

3 Add the egg mixture to the saucepan with the milk, cinnamon stick, and lemon rind. Heat the mixture and allow to simmer, stirring continuously. Make sure that the mixture does not come to a boil. With a slotted spoon, remove and discard the cinnamon stick and lemon rind. Allow to cool, then freeze the mixture until it reaches a creamy consistency. Serve in individual dessert glasses, and decorate with mint.

FLAN DE NARANJAS

Orange Flan

Although meals in Spain usually end with a piece of fresh fruit, Spaniards eagerly consume prepared desserts on special occasions or holidays. Flan, in particular, tops the list of Spanish dessert favorites. While most flans resemble traditional custard desserts, this flan is infused with a delicate orange flavor, a lingering reminder of Spain's Moorish past.

SERVES 4 • 20 MINUTES PREPARATION • 40 MINUTES COOKING

3/4 cup (5 oz/150 g) sugar, for the caramel topping

1/2 cup (4 fl. oz/125 ml) water, for the caramel topping

2 cups (15 fl. oz/450 ml) freshly squeezed orange juice

Grated rind of 1 orange

4 medium eggs

2 medium egg yolks

3/4 cup (5 oz/150 g) sugar

Orange slices, to decorate

1 Preheat the oven to 350 °F (180 °C). To make the caramel topping, heat the sugar and the water in a small saucepan, swirling gently until a golden brown caramel is formed. Immediately divide the mixture evenly among four individual ramekins. Swirl and tilt the ramekins to ensure that the caramel coats the ramekins' sides and bases. Place the ramekins in a baking pan.

2 In a small bowl, bring the orange juice and orange rind to a boil, then remove from the heat. Meanwhile, in a separate bowl, whisk together the eggs and egg yolks with the remaining sugar, until the mixture is thick. Pour in the orange juice and rind, stirring constantly.

3 Divide this mixture among the four ramekins in the baking pan, then pour boiling water around them to create a bain-marie. Bake in the oven for about 25 minutes or until lightly set. Allow to cool, then refrigerate overnight.

4 Immediately before serving, briefly immerse the bases of the ramekins in hot water and, if necessary, pass a knife around the outer edges of the ramekins to make unmolding easier. Inverse and unmold the desserts on to serving saucers. Decorate with fresh orange slices.

ARROZ CON LECHE

Spanish Rice Pudding

Some say that this dessert descends from the Moorish occupation of Spain centuries ago, as may be evidenced by the traditionally Arabic mixture of cinnamon and rice. This creamy dessert may be savored warm or cold, though most Spanish establishments tend to serve it straight from the oven. If you wish, you may decorate the finished pudding with raisins and an extra sprinkling of cinnamon.

SERVES 4 • 15 MINUTES PREPARATION • 25 MINUTES COOKING

2 cups (16 fl. oz/450 ml) milk

1 cinnamon stick

3 strips lemon rind

Pinch of salt

1/2 cup (4 oz/115 g) short-grain white rice

3 medium egg yolks, beaten

1/3 cup (3 oz/90 g) sugar

1/2 stick (2 oz/50 g) butter

1 teaspoon ground nutmeg

1 In a large saucepan, slowly bring the milk, cinnamon stick, strips of lemon rind, and salt to a boil. With a slotted spoon, remove the cinnamon and lemon rind. Stir in the rice and egg yolks, reduce the heat, and allow the rice to simmer for about 15 minutes, stirring constantly.

2 When the rice is soft, add the sugar and butter and combine well. Pour the mixture into a serving dish, sprinkle with nutmeg, and serve warm.

ENSAIMADAS

Majorcan Sweet Bread

A Majorcan favorite, ensaimadas are warm, yeast-based cakes fashioned into round, coiled shapes. Although delicious, these cakes are time-consuming to prepare, because the dough must be allowed to rise several times. Nevertheless, when time is available, these make delightful breakfast rolls. This recipe yields one very large, beautiful coil that can be sliced into individual portions. Serve with hot chocolate or steaming coffee.

SERVES 8 • 50 MINUTES PREPARATION PLUS RISING TIME • 50 MINUTES COOKING

4 teaspoons active dry yeast

1 cup (8 fl. oz/225 ml) milk, warmed

1/2 cup (4 oz/115 g) sugar

1 teaspoon salt

4 1/2 cups (16 oz/450 g) plain flour

2 large eggs

2 tablespoons olive oil

Plain flour, for coating

1 1/2 sticks (6 oz/170 g) butter, softened

Butter, for brushing

Sugar, for dusting

1 Dissolve the yeast in the warmed milk and set aside.

2 Combine the sugar and salt together in a large bowl. Gradually add the flour and warm milk mixture. Blend thoroughly. Add the eggs and olive oil, mix well, and knead until soft and well-blended. Cover with a damp cloth and leave to rise in a warm place for about 1 hour, or until dough has doubled in volume.

3 Knead the dough again, and using a rolling pin, roll the dough as thin as possible over a floured surface. Brush the entire surface of the dough with softened butter.

4 Start rolling the dough, bit by bit, from one side to the other (as if you were rolling up a poster). When the dough has been rolled up, allow it to rest for 1 hour.

5 After the dough has risen, coil it loosely, so that it resembles a snail shell. Transfer the coil to a greased baking sheet. Cover with an extremely large inverted bowl or bucket, large enough to ensure that the dough will not stick to the bowl's surface when it rises. Allow the dough to rise for several hours.

6 Preheat the oven to 375 °F (190 °C). Bake the dough coil for around 45 minutes, or until the top is golden-brown. Brush the surface with melted butter and sprinkle generously with sugar. To serve, cut into slices.

CREMA CATALANA

Sweet Catalan Cream

Because of its crisp, caramelized topping, this creamy Catalan dessert is often compared to the French crème brûlée. Sweet Catalan cream, however, is not as heavy or rich as its French cousin, and thus makes a more pleasant ending to a heavy paella dinner.

SERVES 4 • 15 MINUTES PREPARATION • 15 MINUTES COOKING

2 cups (15 fl. oz/450 ml) milk

1 cinnamon stick

Rind of 1 lemon

1 teaspoon vanilla extract

4 medium egg yolks

1 tablespoon cornflour

1 cup (7 oz/200 g) caster sugar

1 In a saucepan, bring the milk, cinnamon stick, lemon rind, and vanilla extract to a boil. Simmer for several minutes then discard the cinnamon stick and lemon rind. Set the flavored milk aside.

2 In a bowl, whisk the egg yolks together with the cornflour and $3/4$ cup (5 oz/150 g) of the sugar until the mixture is creamy. Gradually pour this mixture into the saucepan with the milk, mixing continuously.

3 Slowly heat the mixture until it begins to thicken, taking care that the mixture does not boil. Pour into four shallow heatproof serving dishes, allow to cool, and refrigerate for several hours.

4 Immediately before serving, preheat the grill and scatter the remaining sugar evenly over each serving. Place the dishes under the grill until the sugar topping begins to caramelize. Remove from the grill and serve.

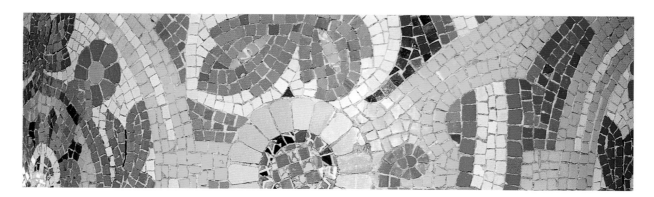

DESSERTS

CHURROS

Deep-fried Spanish Pastry Spirals

Although churros are typically served for breakfast, they also make a good dessert. Like paella, churros are served in different fashions throughout Spain. In Andalucía, for instance, they are usually served with coffee and superfine sugar on the side for dipping. Barcelona typically serves churros with confectioner's sugar, and at least one Barcelona establishment serves churros cold encased in a hard, chocolate shell that melts when dipped into steaming coffee. Madrid's churros are probably the most famous, served with a dense, rich cup of hot chocolate, almost too thick to drink. The Madrileños dip the churros in the thick hot chocolate, which is supposed to be thick enough to hold a spoon.

SERVES 4 • 25 MINUTES PREPARATION • 15 MINUTES COOKING

1³/4 cups (7 oz/200 g) self-raising flour

2 tablespoons sugar

¹/4 teaspoon salt

4 tablespoons olive oil

³/4 cup (6 fl. oz/175 ml) water

1 egg, beaten

Oil, for deep-frying

Caster sugar, for dusting

1 Pass the flour, sugar, and salt through a sifter on to a plate. Set aside. In a saucepan, bring the oil and water to a boil. Remove from the heat and quickly add the flour mixture. Beat vigorously until smooth. Gradually beat in the egg until the mixture forms a smooth, thick paste.

2 Half-fill a large deep skillet suitable for deep-frying with oil and heat to 375 °F (190 °C). Spoon the dough into a pastry bag fitted with a ½–inch (1–cm) nozzle, and pipe three or four pieces of dough into the hot oil, using the nozzle to form the dough into spirals or horseshoe shapes. Fry for 2 to 3 minutes or until golden. Using a slotted spoon, transfer the dough pieces to paper towels and drain.

3 Fry the remaining mixture in the same way. Generously dust all the fried pastries with sugar and serve hot with coffee or hot chocolate.

SANGRÍA DE MOLOCOTÓN Y NARANJA

Peach and Orange Sangria

This sparkling sangría uses white wine instead of red, to better partner the vibrant peaches and oranges. Lemons and cherries may be added too, for an additional splash of color. A bit more potent than its sweet taste suggests, this sangría should be savored slowly.

MAKES 6 GLASSES • 10 MINUTES PREPARATION

3¹/₄ cups (26 fl. oz/750 ml) dry white wine

¹/₃ cup (3 oz/90 g) sugar

¹/₃ cup (5 tablespoons) Triple Sec

¹/₃ cup (5 tablespoons) peach-flavored brandy

2 medium peaches, peeled and sliced

2 medium oranges, sliced thin crosswise

1 cup (8 fl. oz/225 ml) sparkling orange soda

1 cup (8 fl. oz/225 ml) ginger ale

1 In a large serving bowl, combine all the ingredients except the orange soda and ginger ale and mix well. Refrigerate overnight.

2 Immediately before serving, mix in the orange soda and ginger ale. Serve over ice.

SANGRÍA FUERTE

Potent Sangría

For those who like their liquor strong, this powerful sangría aims to please. Fortified with wine, vodka, and gin, this recipe will strip you of your everyday worries (and perhaps, your memory as well). Olé!

MAKES 6 GLASSES • 10 MINUTES PREPARATION

3^{1}/$_{4}$ cups (26 fl. oz/750 ml) dry red wine

2 cups (16 fl. oz/450 ml) sparkling apple juice

4 tablespoons gin

4 tablespoons citron-flavored vodka

2 tablespoons sugar

1 tablespoon orange juice

1 tablespoon lemon juice

1 small orange, sliced thin crosswise

1 small lemon, sliced thin crosswise

1 small lime, sliced thin crosswise

1 Pour all the ingredients into a large pitcher, mix well, and refrigerate. Serve chilled over ice.

SANGRÍA DE TRES FRUTAS

Citrus Sangría

This zesty sangría is especially refreshing thanks to the orange, lemon, and lime. Tangy and sweet, this drink tastes just like summer.

MAKES 6 GLASSES • 10 MINUTES PREPARATION

3³/4 cups (30 fl. oz/900 ml) dry red wine

¹/2 cup (4 fl. oz/125 ml) Cointreau

¹/2 cup (4 fl. oz/125 ml) brandy

Juice of 1 large orange

Juice of 1 medium lemon

Juice of 1 medium lime

3 tablespoons icing sugar

Club soda, to taste

1 small orange, sliced thin crosswise

1 small lemon, sliced thin crosswise

1 small lime, sliced thin crosswise

1 Mix the wine, Cointreau, brandy, citrus juices, and sugar in a large pitcher. Refrigerate overnight.

2 Immediately before serving, add the club soda, orange, lemon, and lime slices. Serve over ice.

SANGRÍA DE FRUTAS

Fruity Sangría

*This simple sangría requires some patience, but minimal effort.
If served at a party, guests will delight in nibbling on the
wine-flavored apple and pear chunks remaining in their cups
after their sangria has vanished.*

MAKES 18 GLASSES • 15 MINUTES PREPARATION

8 cups (64 fl. oz/1.8 l) dry red wine

8 cups (64 fl. oz/1.8 l) apple juice

1 small grapefruit, cut into eighths

1 medium orange, sliced thin crosswise

1 medium lemon, sliced thin crosswise

1 small pear, diced

1 medium apple, diced

1 Combine the wine, apple juice, and grapefruit pieces in a
large pitcher. Mix well, cover, and refrigerate overnight.

2 The following day, add the orange and lemon slices to the
wine. Refrigerate for a further 3 hours.

3 Add the pear and apple to the mixture, then allow to stand
for a further 1 hour to absorb the flavor fully. Mix well and
serve over ice.

SANGRÍA DE ARÁNDANO Y FRESAS

Cranberry and Strawberry Sangría

This playful sangría is sure to become one of your party staples. It is only slightly more tedious to prepare than the other sangrías, but well worth the extra little effort. This fruity, delicious sangría is practically a fiesta in itself but with sangría like this, why wait for guests?

MAKES 8 GLASSES • 15 MINUTES PREPARATION • 5 MINUTES COOKING

1 cup (8 fl. oz/225 ml) water

2/3 cup (5 oz/140 g) sugar

3 cloves

2 medium lemon slices

2 medium lime slices

4 cranberry herbal tea bags

3 1/4 cups (26 fl. oz/750 ml) dry white wine

2 cups (16 fl. oz/450 ml) cranberry juice

6 tablespoons brandy

2 tablespoons Triple Sec

1 large orange, cut into chunks

1 1/4 cups (5 oz/140 g) fresh strawberries, trimmed

1 cup (8 fl. oz/225 ml) club soda

1 Combine the water, sugar, cloves, and lemon and lime slices together in a saucepan and set over medium heat. Mix well and allow to simmer for a couple of minutes. Reduce the heat to low, and simmer for a further 2 to 3 minutes.

2 Remove the saucepan from the heat and add in the tea bags. After allowing the tea bags to infuse for five minutes, remove and discard the tea bags and the cloves, and transfer the mixture to a large serving pitcher. Add the wine, cranberry juice, brandy, and Triple Sec. Mix well and drop in the orange chunks and strawberries. Cover and refrigerate for at least 12 hours.

3 Immediately before serving, mix in the club soda for extra fizz. Serve chilled, over ice.

SANGRIA

SANGRÍA BLANCA

White Sangría

Bursting with sparkling flavor, this clear version of sangría is unique in its use of ice cubes made from apple juice. For parties, this can be served in a large, transparent punch bowl next to a transparent bowl containing traditional red sangría. This pairing provides a beautiful contrast, provided they are not immediately consumed by eager guests, as is often the case.

MAKES 8 GLASSES • 15 MINUTES PREPARATION

Apple juice, for ice cubes

1¼ cups (10 fl. oz/300 ml) water

1 small bunch fresh mint

½ cup (3½ oz/100g) sugar

3 cinnamon sticks

3¼ cups (26 fl. oz/750 ml) dry white wine

2 medium peaches, peeled, pitted, and sliced

2 small pears, cut into chunks

2 medium oranges, sliced crosswise

2 small lemons, sliced crosswise

3 cups (24 fl. oz/700 ml) sparkling apple cider

Mint leaves, to garnish (optional)

1 To make the apple-juice ice cubes, pour the apple juice into two ice trays and freeze until the sangría is ready to serve.

2 Combine the water, mint leaves, sugar, and cinnamon in a small saucepan, and bring to a boil over medium heat. Reduce the heat and simmer for several minutes. Remove from the heat and allow to cool. Once the mixture has cooled to room temperature, remove and discard the mint and cinnamon sticks. Transfer the remaining mixture to a large serving bowl.

3 Add the wine, peaches, pears, and the orange and lemon slices to the serving bowl. Mix well, cover, and refrigerate overnight. Immediately before serving, mix in the sparkling apple cider and the apple-juice ice cubes. Garnish with fresh mint leaves, if desired.

SANGRÍA CLARA

White Sangría

White sangría may seem more pure than the original red version, but it is every bit as potent. Here, the fresh mint leaves infuse the sangría with an unforgettable zesty freshness. The most delicious ingredients in this recipe, however, are the peaches, which tend to absorb the perfect amount of white wine.

MAKES 8 GLASSES • 15 MINUTES PREPARATION

1 cup (8 fl. oz/225 ml) water

1 small bunch fresh mint

1/2 cup (31/2 oz/100 g) sugar

3 cloves

4 short cinnamon sticks

31/4 cups (26 fl. oz/750 ml) dry white wine

2 cups (16 fl. oz/450 ml) sparkling apple cider

1/2 cup (4 fl. oz/125 ml) orange juice

2 small oranges, sliced thin crosswise

2 small apples, cut into chunks

2 small peaches, peeled and cut into chunks

1 In a small saucepan, combine the water, mint, sugar, cloves, and cinnamon sticks over medium heat. Allow to simmer for about 5 minutes. Remove from the heat, and allow the mixture to cool down to room temperature.

2 Remove and discard the mint leaves, cloves, and cinnamon sticks, and pour the mixture into a large serving pitcher. Mix in all of the remaining ingredients, cover, and refrigerate overnight.

3 Serve the following day over ice.

SANGRÍA DE FIESTA
Party Sangría

Fiesta sangría is a popular choice for parties, and almost everyone partaking of it is bound to find at least several delicious fruit slices bobbing around in their cup. This sangría is also especially attractive served in a wine glass with an orange slice garnishing the rim.

MAKES 4 GLASSES • 10 MINUTES PREPARATION

3 1/4 cups (26 fl. oz/750 ml) dry red wine

1/3 cup (3 oz/90 g) sugar

1/3 cup (5 tablespoons) brandy

1/3 cup (5 tablespoons) Cointreau

1/3 cup (5 tablespoons) lemon-flavored vodka

1 small lemon, sliced thin crosswise

1 small orange, sliced thin crosswise

1 small lime, sliced thin crosswise

1 medium pear, diced

1 medium peach, peeled and sliced

2 cups (8oz/220 g) sliced strawberries

1 bottle carbonated lemon-lime soda

1 In a large serving bowl, combine all ingredients except the strawberries and soda. Chill in the refrigerator overnight.

2 Immediately before serving, stir in the strawberries and lemon-lime soda. Pour into chilled glasses and serve.

SANGRÍA PICANTE
Spicy Sangría

This white sangría has a definite kick, and is thus not for those who prefer a milder, more mellow version of the refreshment. Imbibe accordingly—and have plenty of iced water on hand!

MAKES 6 GLASSES • 10 MINUTES PREPARATION

3 3/4 cups (30 fl. oz/900 ml) dry white wine

3 tablespoons brandy

2 small red chillies, seeded and quartered

2 medium tart green apples, diced

2 medium peaches, peeled, pitted, and sliced

2 large yellow plums, peeled, pitted, and sliced

1 cup (8 fl. oz/225 ml) club soda

1 Combine all ingredients except the club soda in a large serving pitcher and refrigerate overnight.

2 The following day, immediately before serving, mix in the club soda for added fizz. Serve over ice.

SANGRÍA TRADICIONAL
Basic Sangría

A very simple, unfussy sangría. While this sangría is delicious as is, this recipe intentionally leaves ample room for improvisation and additions, and should therefore be used as a springboard to create your own unique sangría recipes. The unaltered recipe below, however, would meet with the approval of strict sangría traditionalists.

MAKES 4 GLASSES • 10 MINUTES PREPARATION

3^1/$_4$ cups (26 fl. oz/750 ml) dry red wine

1 tablespoon sugar

Juice of 1 large orange

Juice of 1 large lemon

1 large orange, sliced thin crosswise

1 large lemon, sliced thin crosswise

2 medium peaches, peeled, pitted, and cut into chunks

1 cup (8 fl. oz/225 ml) club soda

1 Combine all ingredients except for the club soda in a large punch bowl or serving pitcher, mixing well. Refrigerate overnight. Immediately before serving, mix in the club soda for added fizz. Ladle into cups with ice cubes.